A Vegan Taste of Mexico

A Vegan Taste of Mexico

Linda Majzlik

JON CARPENTER

Our books may be ordered from bookshops or (post free in the UK) from
Jon Carpenter Publishing, Alder House, Market Street, Charlbury,
England OX7 3PH

Please send for a catalogue

Credit card orders should be phoned or faxed to 01689 870437
or 01608 811969

First published in 2002 by
Jon Carpenter Publishing
Alder House, Market Street, Charlbury, England OX7 3PH
☎ 01608 811969

Reprinted 2004

ISBN 1 897766 71 8

Printed in England by J. W. Arrowsmith Ltd., Bristol

CONTENTS

Vegetables

Salads

Desserts

Baking

Drinks

INTRODUCTION

L ying between the United States to the north and the Central American countries to the south, Mexico enjoys a mixed climate, with both tropical and temperate conditions. The agricultural land in the more temperate north of the country is used to grow staples such as corn and wheat, while the south is ideally suitable for growing tropical fruits and vegetables.

Before the great Aztec empire was defeated by the Spanish Conquistadores in the early sixteenth century, the native diet consisted mainly of avocados, beans, chillis, chocolate, nuts, peppers, potatoes, seeds, squashes, sweetcorn and tomatoes. The Spanish invaders introduced new foods such as rice and wheat and planted fruits and vegetables that reminded them of home. They were also responsible for taking Mexican food plants back to Europe for cultivation there. The native Mexicans readily incorporated the new foods into their diet and today their colourful and wholesome style of cooking reflects its foundations in their old world coupled with the influence of the European settlers.

The eating pattern of the modern-day Mexican may seem excessive to outsiders, but eating is a serious business in Mexico and a large part of the day can be devoted to preparation and cooking and finally eating. A typical day might begin with a light breakfast, *desayuno*, of hot chocolate and pan dulce or tortillas. A mid-morning brunch-type meal, *almuerzo*, follows, maybe coffee with tortillas and beans and fresh fruit. The main meal of the day, *comida*, is a leisurely affair taken around mid-afternoon and consisting of several courses. The meal begins with little appetisers, *bocadillos*, then 'wet soup', *sopa aguada*, followed by 'dry soup', *sopa seca*, which may be a rice, pasta or noodle dish. The main course, *platos fuertes*, is served with accompaniments such as salad, salsa, tortillas and beans, and is followed by dessert, *postres*, although after such a hearty meal fresh fruits, ice creams or fruit sorbets are usually preferred to heavier puddings. The meal is rounded off with coffee or hot chocolate. Understandably, a little siesta is normally taken at the end of this marathon meal. Later on in the evening a supper, *merienda*, of a light tortilla-based snack is all that is usually required.

Many festivals and patriotic holidays are celebrated throughout the year and naturally enough food takes centre stage, with dishes specially prepared for the celebrations. Foods which display the colours of the Mexican flag are favourites for Mexican Independence Day.

If you don't want to follow the Mexican meal plan, all recipes can be fitted neatly into other less excessive eating patterns. Lots of dishes can also be made in advance and frozen, and these lend themselves admirably to serving at parties and buffets.

The Mexican style of cooking can be very frugal and nothing is ever wasted. Stale tortillas find their way into soups and casseroles and leftover beans and vegetables will be wrapped in tortillas and eaten at other meals. With its emphasis on fresh fruits and vegetables, grains, beans and lentils, nuts and seeds, this vibrant and nutritious cuisine is one which should appeal greatly to vegans.

THE VEGAN MEXICAN STORECUPBOARD

Colourful, wholesome and authentic-tasting Mexican fare can be easily prepared with fresh vegetables and fruit and some of the following ingredients from the storecupboard.

Agar agar A vegan gelling compound made from various types of seaweed. Used as an alternative to gelatine when making fruit jellies.

Almonds These may not be used as regularly as other nuts, but ground almonds are an essential ingredient in mole sauce and chopped flaked almonds add crunchiness to savoury soya mince.

Avocado Grown widely in Mexico, avocados are used extensively in cooking, as well as being exported to other countries. The avocado is highly nutritious, containing good amounts of vitamins and minerals. When ripe, the flesh around the neck of the pears should yield to gentle pressure. Unripe avocados keep well in the fridge for up to 2 weeks. To ripen, keep at room temperature for 2-3 days. Ripe avocados can be stored in the fridge for a couple of days to prevent them ripening further. Cut avocados need to be sprinkled with lemon or lime juice to stop the flesh discolouring.

Beans and chickpeas Staple and nutritious ingredients, used both in countless savoury recipes and simply on their own as an accompaniment. Red kidney, pinto, borlotti and black beans are all popular varieties and along with chickpeas are worth cooking in bulk and freezing. Tinned beans and chickpeas are a useful standby.

Breadcrumbs White bread and cornbread crumbs are used for toppings and as ingredients in savoury dishes. Breadcrumbs can easily be made by whizzing bread in a food processor or nutmill until crumbled. Breadcrumbs can be stored in the freezer and used from frozen.

Capers The small green flower buds from a trailing bush, capers have a piquant taste and are sold preserved in either vinegar or brine. They are used as an ingredient and for garnishing.

Cheese Numerous recipes require cheese and vegan 'Cheddar'-type versions are used here. Some brands melt more easily than others, so it is a good idea to experiment.

Chillis A crucial ingredient. There are believed to be about a hundred Mexican varieties alone, which vary in size, colour and strength. Some of the better known Mexican varieties are jalapeno, poblano and serrano. Fresh chillis store well in the fridge for about 7-10 days. Bottled chillis are also available and these are used in a variety of recipes or just served separately as a condiment. As well as adding 'heat' and flavour to dishes, chillis contain a good amount of nutrients and are an effective decongestant.

Chocolate Mexicans are extremely fond of chocolate and chocolate-flavoured desserts are very popular, as is hot chocolate, which is drunk throughout the day and often after meals instead of coffee. The famous Mexican mole sauce includes chocolate as an ingredient.

Cocoa powder Made from roasted and ground cocoa beans, cocoa powder is used in various dessert, baking and drinks recipes. Cocoa beans were highly prized by ancient Mexican civilizations and used as currency.

Cornflour A very fine starchy white flour which is milled from corn. It is sometimes known as cornstarch and is used to thicken sauces.

Cornmeal Ground corn which is milled in various grades from fine to coarse. Also known as maizemeal, it is used for cornbread and cornmeal pie.

Cream cheese There are some very good non-dairy alternatives to cream cheese which are made from soya. Choose unflavoured varieties for use in both sweet and savoury recipes.

Flour With the introduction of wheat by the Spanish invaders, Mexicans were able to make tortillas from flour and so add considerably to their repertoire of dishes. Wheat tortillas made from plain white flour are more pliable than those made with corn and they are used extensively to enclose savoury and sweet fillings.

Herbs The Spanish influence on Mexican cuisine is clearly evident in the types of herbs used, most of which are native plants of the Mediterranean region. They are mainly used fresh, but occasionally dried.

Bay leaves These dark green, aromatic leaves from an evergreen tree are best used dried to impart their distinct, strong and slightly bitter flavour. They are used in various soups and main course recipes. Ground bay leaves are used to obtain a more concentrated flavour.

Coriander Without a doubt coriander is the most popular Mexican herb. This uniquely flavoured herb is used in a whole host of recipes, as an ingredient and as garnish. It is always used fresh.

Oregano Sometimes referred to as wild marjoram, oregano is a small-leafed herb that has a natural affinity with tomatoes.

Parsley This universally popular herb is used both as an ingredient and for garnishing.

Thyme A small-leafed, highly aromatic herb which gives a wonderful aroma when added to roasted vegetables. Fresh or dried thyme is also added to various soups and savoury dishes.

Lentils Brown and red lentils are used in a variety of main course and soup recipes. Both combine well with other ingredients and are a rich source of protein, fibre, vitamins and minerals.

Masa harina Specially prepared fine flour milled from dried corn and used to make corn tortillas.

Olives Olive trees are believed to have been planted by the Spanish invaders to remind them of home. Green olives are preferred by Mexicans and these are used as a garnish or as an ingredient.

Parmesan An authentic-tasting vegan version made from soya is available from health food stores and some supermarkets. It is used as a garnish for soups and a topping for other savoury dishes.

Pasta and noodles Small pasta shapes and thin noodles are combined with other ingredients to make delicious soups and main courses. Read the ingredients label on the packet before buying as some varieties contain eggs.

Peanuts A native Mexican ingredient which is a good source of protein, minerals and vitamins. Roasted peanuts are a popular snack, while ground peanuts are used as an ingredient and toasted they are used as garnish.

Pecans The smooth glossy shell of this native nut contains the pecan kernel, which looks very much like a walnut but has a sweeter, less bitter taste. Pecans are used extensively in Mexico, both in sweet and savoury recipes and for garnishing. Although pecans are rich in nutrients they also have a very high fat content, so it might be wise to use them in moderation.

Pine kernels These tiny fragrant nuts with a sweet creamy taste are the seeds of a variety of pine tree. Their flavour is enhanced if lightly toasted and they are often used as a garnish.

Pomegranate The seeds of the pomegranate are often used as a crunchy garnish for fruit and vegetable salads. The fruit is ripe when the hard, rubbery skin is blushed with red. Unpeeled pomegranates will keep for several weeks in the fridge.

Pumpkin seeds These pale green seeds are a very rich source of iron. They are enjoyed roasted as a snack and ground as an ingredient in savoury puddings and sauces, and they are also used as an attractive and nutritious garnish.

Rice A staple food in the Mexican diet since it was introduced by the Spanish in the early sixteenth century. Long grain white rice is preferred and this is eaten as 'dry soup', main course, accompaniment or dessert.

Sesame seeds A vital ingredient in mole sauce, sesame seeds are packed with nutrition. They are often sprinkled on sweet and savoury breads and tortillas before baking, or toasted and used as a garnish for a variety of savoury dishes.

Soya milk Unsweetened soya milk has been used in both sweet and savoury recipes.

Spices Compared to other cuisines from around the world, Mexicans do not use a great variety of spices. Those that are used however are considered essential in some dishes.

Black pepper An essential seasoning in savoury dishes. Coarsely-ground black peppercorns are preferred to ready-ground pepper.

Cayenne pepper The dried fruit of a hot red pepper. Deep red in colour and very pungent, cayenne is used to add 'heat' to a dish.

Chilli powder Used to add 'heat' to many dishes.

Cinnamon The dried, inner bark of a tree of the laurel family. This highly pungent, yet comforting, mild sweet spice is very popular in Mexican cooking. It is mainly used in sweet dishes, but occasionally also added to savoury recipes. Cinnamon sticks are traditionally used to stir hot chocolate and coffee-flavoured drinks.

Coriander The dried seed of the coriander plant, which belongs to the parsley family. Ground coriander has a mild, sweet, orangey flavour.

Cumin Ground cumin is used more frequently than seeds. Its strong earthy flavour combines well with tomatoes and it is probably the most widely used spice in Mexican savoury recipes.

Paprika Made from the dried fruit of a sweet red pepper. Mild and slightly sweet in flavour, paprika is often added to dishes containing tomatoes.

Sweetcorn A fundamental ingredient, which has been grown in Mexico since ancient times. Corn is used in some form or other in all manner of dishes, from starters to desserts, and it adds a good source of fibre, vitamins and minerals to the diet. Fresh sweetcorn is preferred, but frozen or tinned kernels can be used instead.

Tabasco sauce A very hot piquant sauce made from tabasco chillies which have been steeped in vinegar and matured in casks for several years.

Tamarind The fruit of a large tropical tree, tamarind is used to add sourness to savoury dishes. It is usually sold in a sticky block consisting of crushed pods, which needs to be soaked in hot water to produce a purée. Jars of ready-made purée are also available.

Textured vegetable protein A nutritious and versatile soya product, which readily absorbs the flavours of other ingredients. The natural minced variety is used here in various savoury recipes.

Tinned tomatoes Crushed tinned tomatoes are used in preference to fresh where a stronger tomato flavour is required.

Tomato purée Used to strengthen the flavour of and add colour to tomato-based dishes. Tomato purée should be used sparingly – too much can give a slightly acidic taste.

Vegetable oils Corn and olive oils are preferred for frying, both of which are believed to lower cholesterol levels. Olive oil is used in salad dressings.

Vegetable stock Used in a variety of savoury recipes, home-made vegetable stock adds a more authentic flavour than stock cubes. It can be made in bulk and frozen in measured quantities. Peel and chop a selection of vegetables such as carrots, celery, courgette, green beans, onions, potatoes and sweet potatoes. Put them in a large pan with a couple of chopped garlic cloves and a chopped green chilli, a few sprigs of fresh parsley and a bay leaf. Cover with water and bring to the boil, cover and simmer for 30 minutes. Strain the liquid through a fine sieve.

Vinegar Red and white wine vinegars are used for making salad dressings.

Walnuts Although not as popular as pecans, walnuts are very similar and may be substituted in recipes calling for pecans. Walnuts combine well with vegetables and when ground can form the basis of savoury sauces. They may even be healthier than pecans, as some studies have found that the fatty acids in walnuts can help lower cholesterol levels.

Yeast Easy-blend dried yeast is used in the recipes requiring yeast. It does not need to be reconstituted in liquid.

BASIC RECIPES

Along with certain sauces and guacamole, the following are used over and over again to create various Mexican dishes. Tortillas, the 'bread of Mexico', freeze very well, so for convenience it is worth making these in bulk. Depending on how they are filled, folded and cooked, tortillas are transformed into a multitude of snacks, light meals and main courses and sweetened versions are eaten for dessert. No food is ever wasted and even stale tortillas will be used up in an inventive way.

Beans are the mainstay of Mexican cuisine and a large pot of beans is invariably simmering away on the cooker. They are served at almost every meal, in combination with other ingredients, refried, or simply just as a side dish. Savoury soya mince is another useful recipe, which again can be frozen. It is frequently used as a filling or topping for tortillas, served on its own, or with rice as a main course.

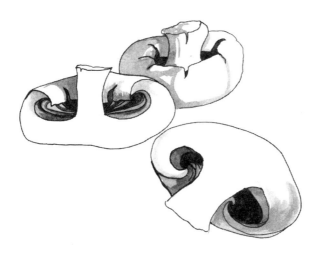

Corn tortillas

(makes 8 6 inch/15cm or 20 4 inch/10cm tortillas)

These savoury pancakes are traditionally flattened and shaped by hand, but many Mexican cooks now use a special tortilla press to speed up the process. Using sheets of greaseproof paper and the bottom of a pan to flatten the dough is a good substitute for a press. A non-stick pan is essential when cooking the tortillas and care should be taken not to overheat the pan as tortillas burn easily. Simply wrap the cooked tortillas in foil or cling film to freeze. To reheat from frozen, wrap them in foil and place in a moderate oven for 10-15 minutes until hot. Both corn and wheat tortillas are always eaten hot.

> 8oz/225g masa harina
> 2oz/50g plain flour
> pinch of salt
> approx. 7 fl.oz/200ml hot water

Mix the masa harina with the flour and salt and gradually add the water until a firm dough forms. Knead the dough well, then divide into 8 or 20 equal portions depending on the size of tortilla required.

For the larger tortillas cut 16 pieces of greaseproof paper of about 7 inches/18cm square, for the smaller tortillas 40 pieces of about 5 inches/13cm square.

Take a portion of dough and roll it into a ball. Put this in the centre of a piece of greaseproof paper and place another sheet on the top. Press firmly down on the dough with a saucepan until it is either about 6 inches/15cm or 4 inches/10cm in diameter, depending on which size you are making. Make all the tortillas in the same way, leaving them in between the greaseproof paper until ready to cook.

Heat a heavy-based non-stick frying pan until hot. Carefully peel off one of the pieces of paper and invert the tortilla into the hot pan. Then remove the other piece of paper and cook the tortilla for 30-60 seconds until it is lightly browned underneath and the edges start to lift. Turn it over and cook the other side. Stack the cooked tortillas on a plate and cover with kitchen paper or a clean cloth.

Wheat tortillas   *(makes 8)*

Tortillas made from flour come from the northern part of Mexico. They are softer and traditionally larger than corn tortillas, but are cooked on a griddle in the same way. Wheat tortillas need to be interleaved with greaseproof paper when they are to be frozen to prevent them sticking together. Reheat frozen wheat tortillas in the same way as corn tortillas.

> 8oz/225g plain flour
>
> 2oz/50g vegan margarine or 4 tablespoons corn oil
>
> 1 teaspoon salt
>
> approx. 3 fl.oz/75ml warm water

Sift the flour and salt into a mixing bowl and rub in the margarine or stir in the oil. Gradually add the water until a soft dough forms. Turn out onto a floured board and knead well. Divide the dough into 8 equal pieces, roll each piece into a ball and roll these out very thinly on a floured board into a circle of about 7 inches/18cm. Keep each tortilla covered with kitchen paper or a clean cloth while making the next one so that they do not dry out.

Heat a heavy-based non-stick frying pan until hot. Carefully place a tortilla in the pan, making sure it lies flat. Cook for about 40 seconds until lightly browned underneath, then turn over and cook the other side. Transfer to a plate and keep covered until all the tortillas are made.

Frijoles

1lb/450g dried beans (e.g. red kidney, pinto or black)

1 onion, peeled and chopped

2 garlic cloves, crushed

1 green chilli, finely chopped

2 sprigs of fresh parsley

Wash the beans thoroughly, put them in a large pan and cover with water. Put the lid on the pan and leave the beans to soak overnight. Add the remaining ingredients and bring to the boil. Cover and simmer for about an hour and a half until the beans are tender, keeping the water level up by adding boiling water when needed. Drain the beans and keep the cooking liquid, as this can be used as stock for other recipes.

Refried beans

1lb/450g drained cooked beans

1 red onion, peeled and finely chopped

2 garlic cloves, crushed

2 tablespoons corn oil

1 rounded dessertspoon vegan margarine

1 tablespoon water

Heat the oil and gently fry the onion and garlic until soft. Remove from the heat, add the beans and mash smooth, then return to the heat and add the margarine and water. Heat while stirring continuously for 5-10 minutes until the mixture is almost dry.

Savoury soya mince

14oz/400g tin crushed tomatoes

4oz/100g natural minced textured vegetable protein

4oz/100g red pepper, finely chopped

1oz/25g raisins, chopped

1oz/25g flaked almonds, chopped

1 onion, peeled and finely chopped

2 garlic cloves, crushed

1 red chilli, finely chopped

10 fl.oz/300ml vegetable stock

1 tablespoon corn oil

1 tablespoon red wine vinegar

1 dessertspoon tomato purée

1 teaspoon demerara sugar

1 teaspoon paprika

pinch of ground cinnamon

black pepper

Heat the oil and gently soften the onion, garlic and chilli. Add the remaining ingredients apart from the flaked almonds and stir well. Bring to the boil, then cover and simmer for 15 minutes, stirring occasionally. Remove the lid and continue simmering for another 5 minutes, stirring frequently, until the mixture is thick. Remove from the heat and stir in the almonds.

SOUPS

It would be unthinkable for Mexicans not to have soup as part of the main meal of the day. Whether it is a simple light stock served with salsa or a hearty thick mixture made with vegetables, beans and pasta, soup is an integral part of the main meal. There are two types of Mexican soup, sopa aguada ('wet soup'), which is the more familiar, and sopa seca ('dry soup'). 'Dry soups' can consist of savoury rice dishes or pasta or noodles cooked in tomato-based sauces and garnished with salsa and grated cheese. These are often served as well as 'wet soups', before the main course.

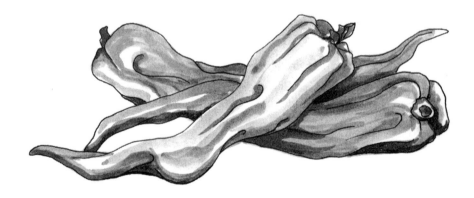

Sweet potato and lentil soup   *(serves 4)*

12oz/350g sweet potato, peeled and diced

4oz/100g red lentils

4oz/100g tomato, skinned and chopped

1 red onion, peeled and finely chopped

1 small red chilli, finely chopped

1 garlic clove, crushed

1 dessertspoon corn oil

30 fl.oz/900ml vegetable stock

½ teaspoon paprika

black pepper

fresh coriander leaves

Heat the oil in a large pan and fry the onion, chilli and garlic until soft. Add the tomato and cook until pulpy. Stir in the lentils, stock and paprika and season with black pepper. Bring to the boil, cover and simmer for 15 minutes, then add the potato and continue simmering for another 20 minutes or so until the potato is cooked. Ladle half of the soup into a blender and blend until smooth. Pour back into the rest of the soup and stir well. Reheat, whilst stirring, then spoon into bowls and garnish each bowl with a few coriander leaves.

Tortilla soup   *(serves 4)*

24 tortilla chips (see page 37)

1 quantity tomato sauce (see page 41)

6oz/175g leek, trimmed and thinly sliced

4oz/100g sweetcorn kernels

4oz/100g carrot, scraped and chopped

4oz/100g green beans, trimmed and chopped

1 red onion, peeled and finely chopped

2 garlic cloves, crushed

1 tablespoon corn oil

6 fl.oz/175ml vegetable stock

grated vegan 'cheese'

chopped pecans

Heat the oil in a large pan and gently fry the leek, onion and garlic. Add the stock, together with the sweetcorn, carrot and green beans. Stir well, bring to the boil and simmer for 5 minutes, then add the tomato sauce and continue simmering, stirring occasionally, for 10 minutes until the mixture is thick and the vegetables are tender. Stir in the tortilla chips and simmer for a couple of minutes more. The tortillas should retain some 'bite' and not be allowed to become soggy. Ladle the soup into bowls and sprinkle with grated 'cheese' and chopped pecans.

Potato, leek and macaroni soup   *(serves 4)*

1lb/450g potatoes, peeled and diced

12oz/350g leek, trimmed and sliced

2oz/50g small macaroni

1 garlic clove, crushed

1 dessertspoon corn oil

1 rounded tablespoon chopped fresh parsley

black pepper

22 fl.oz/650ml vegetable stock

grated vegan 'cheddar'

chopped walnuts

4 fresh parsley sprigs

Fry the leek and garlic in the oil for 5 minutes. Add the potato, chopped parsley and stock and season with black pepper. Stir well and bring to the boil, then cover and simmer for 10 minutes, stirring occasionally. Add the macaroni, cover and continue simmering for about 10 minutes until the macaroni is cooked and the soup is thick. Spoon into serving bowls and sprinkle with grated 'cheddar' and walnuts. Garnish each bowl with a sprig of parsley.

Sweet pepper, tomato and orange soup   (*serves 4*)

1lb/450g mixed peppers (e.g. red, yellow, green, orange), chopped

1lb/450g ripe tomatoes, skinned and chopped

10 fl.oz/300ml fresh orange juice

1 red onion, peeled and finely chopped

1 red chilli, finely chopped

2 garlic cloves, crushed

2 tablespoons corn oil

1 dessertspoon tomato purée

1 dessertspoon demerara sugar

1 teaspoon ground coriander

1 bay leaf

black pepper

chopped capers

Heat the oil in a large pan and gently fry the peppers, onion, chilli and garlic for 5 minutes. Add the remaining ingredients except the capers and stir well. Bring to the boil, cover and simmer for about 15 minutes, stirring occasionally, until the peppers are tender. Ladle into bowls and garnish with chopped capers.

Chilled avocado soup   (*serves 4*)

1 large avocado, peeled and chopped

10 fl.oz/300ml vegetable stock

10 fl.oz/300ml soya milk

2 tablespoons lime juice

black pepper

fresh coriander leaves

Put the avocado, stock, soya milk and lime juice in a blender, season with black pepper and blend until smooth. Chill for a couple of hours. Garnish each bowl of soup with fresh coriander leaves.

Lentil and bean soup *(serves 4)*

4oz/100g red lentils

4oz/100g cooked mixed beans

4oz/100g carrot, scraped and finely chopped

4oz/100g courgette, chopped

4oz/100g leek, trimmed and sliced

4oz/100g mushrooms, wiped and chopped

½ quantity tomato sauce (see page 41)

1 red onion, peeled and finely chopped

1 garlic clove, crushed

16 fl.oz/475ml vegetable stock

1 tablespoon corn oil

1 bay leaf

½ teaspoon chilli powder

grated vegan 'cheese'

Heat the oil and gently fry the onion, leek and garlic until softened. Add the lentils and 12 fl.oz/350ml of vegetable stock and bring to the boil, cover and simmer for 10 minutes. Add the vegetables, tomato sauce, bay leaf, chilli powder and remaining stock, cover again and continue simmering for another 10 minutes. Stir in the beans and simmer covered for 5 minutes more, until the vegetables are done and the soup is thick. Stir frequently to prevent sticking. Sprinkle each bowl of soup with grated 'cheese'.

Aubergine, tomato and pasta soup   *(serves 4)*

8oz/225g aubergine, diced

14oz/400g tin crushed tomatoes

4oz/100g small pasta shapes

1 red onion, peeled and finely chopped

1 red chilli, finely chopped

2 garlic cloves, crushed

15 fl.oz/450ml vegetable stock

2 tablespoons olive oil

1 dessertspoon tamarind purée

1 tablespoon finely chopped fresh oregano

½ teaspoon paprika

1 bay leaf

black pepper

vegan 'Parmesan'

chopped fresh parsley

Fry the aubergine, onion, chilli and garlic in the oil for 10 minutes, stirring regularly to prevent sticking. Dissolve the tamarind purée in the stock and add to the pan together with the tomatoes, pasta, oregano, paprika and bay leaf. Season with black pepper and stir well, then bring to the boil, cover and simmer for about 20 minutes until the soup is thick, stirring occasionally. Ladle into bowls and garnish each bowl with 'Parmesan' and chopped parsley.

Sweetcorn soup   *(serves 4)*

12oz/350g sweetcorn kernels

1 onion, peeled and chopped

1 small red chilli, finely chopped

1 dessertspoon corn oil

20 fl.oz/600ml vegetable stock

5 fl.oz/150ml soya milk

1 bay leaf

black pepper

chopped fresh parsley

Gently fry the onion and chilli in the oil until soft. Add 8oz/225g of the sweetcorn, the stock and the bay leaf and season with black pepper. Bring to the boil, cover and simmer for 10 minutes. Allow to cool slightly, then blend until smooth. Return to the pan and add the remaining corn and the soya milk. Mix well and simmer for a few minutes whilst stirring. Ladle into bowls and garnish with chopped parsley when serving.

Avocado and leek soup *(serves 4)*

1 large avocado, peeled and chopped

8oz/225g leek, trimmed and sliced

1 celery stick, trimmed and sliced

1 garlic clove, crushed

1 tablespoon corn oil

1 teaspoon dried parsley

1 bay leaf

black pepper

22 fl.oz/650ml vegetable stock

4 fl.oz/125ml soya milk

chopped fresh coriander leaves

Heat the oil in a pan and fry the leek, celery and garlic for 5 minutes. Add the remaining ingredients apart from the soya milk and coriander and stir well. Bring to the boil, cover and simmer for 10-15 minutes until the vegetables are tender. Remove the bay leaf and let the soup cool slightly, then blend until smooth. Pour back into the cleaned pan and add the soya milk, stir well and reheat. Garnish each bowl of soup with chopped fresh coriander.

Broad bean and potato soup   *(serves 4)*

8oz/225g shelled broad beans

8oz/225g potato, scraped and diced

1 onion, peeled and finely chopped

1 green chilli, finely chopped

1 dessertspoon corn oil

25 fl.oz/750ml vegetable stock

2 rounded tablespoons finely chopped fresh parsley

1 bay leaf

black pepper

grated vegan 'cheese'

Gently fry the onion and chilli in the oil until softened. Add the remaining ingredients, except the 'cheese', and stir well. Bring to the boil, cover and simmer for 20 minutes. Allow to cool slightly, then blend half of the mixture until smooth. Return it to the pan and stir well. Reheat before serving and sprinkle each bowl of soup with grated 'cheese'.

Courgette, mushroom and vermicelli soup

(serves 4)

8oz/225g courgette, chopped

6oz/175g mushrooms, wiped and chopped

2oz/50g vermicelli, broken

1 onion, peeled and chopped

1 green chilli, chopped

1 garlic clove, chopped

20 fl.oz/600ml vegetable stock

1 dessertspoon corn oil

1 bay leaf

sprig of fresh thyme

black pepper

vegan 'Parmesan'

chopped fresh parsley

Fry the onion, chilli and garlic in the oil until soft. Add the courgettes, stock, bay leaf and thyme and season with black pepper. Stir well and bring to the boil, cover and simmer for 10 minutes. Allow to cool slightly, then discard the thyme and blend the soup until smooth. Return to the rinsed out pan and add the mushrooms and vermicelli. Stir well and simmer for about 5 minutes until the vermicelli and mushrooms are soft. Ladle into bowls and garnish with 'Parmesan' and chopped parsley.

Brown lentil and pecan soup   *(serves 4)*

8oz/225g brown lentils

8oz/225g carrot, scraped and grated

4oz/100g mushrooms, wiped and chopped

2oz/50g pecans, finely grated

1 onion, peeled and finely chopped

2 garlic cloves, crushed

1 tablespoon corn oil

50 fl.oz/1½ litre vegetable stock

2 rounded teaspoons ground cumin

1 rounded teaspoon chilli powder

2 tablespoons finely chopped fresh coriander

black pepper

chopped pecans

Heat the oil in a large pan and gently fry the onion, garlic and carrot for 5 minutes. Add the remaining ingredients apart from the grated and chopped pecans and stir well. Bring to the boil, cover and simmer for 30 minutes. Stir in the grated pecans and continue simmering, stirring occasionally, for 15-20 minutes until the lentils are soft and the mixture is thick. Spoon the soup into bowls and serve garnished with chopped pecans.

Tomato and noodle soup   *(serves 4)*

1lb/450g ripe tomatoes, skinned and chopped

1 red onion, peeled and chopped

1 garlic clove, crushed

1 dessertspoon olive oil

1 dessertspoon tomato purée

1 dessertspoon tamarind purée

1 rounded teaspoon demerara sugar

½ teaspoon dried thyme

½ teaspoon paprika

¼ teaspoon chilli powder

black pepper

2oz/50g thin noodles, broken

20 fl.oz/600ml vegetable stock

chopped fresh coriander leaves

Heat the oil and soften the onion and garlic, then add the tomatoes and cook until pulpy. Dissolve the tomato and tamarind purées in the stock and add to the pan together with the sugar, thyme, paprika and chilli powder. Season with black pepper and pour into a blender. Blend until smooth, then return to the pan and add the noodles. Bring to the boil, cover and simmer for 5-10 minutes, stirring occasionally, until the noodles are soft. Garnish each bowl of soup with chopped coriander.

Black bean, leek and mushroom soup   *(serves 4)*

8oz/225g cooked black beans

8oz/225g leek, trimmed and finely sliced

8oz/225g mushrooms, wiped and chopped

2 garlic cloves, crushed

1 tablespoon corn oil

24 fl.oz/725ml vegetable stock

sprig of fresh thyme

black pepper

chopped fresh parsley

Gently fry the leek, mushrooms and garlic for 5 minutes in the oil. Add the beans, stock and thyme and season with black pepper, then bring to the boil, cover and simmer for 10 minutes. Allow to cool slightly and discard the thyme. Pour half of the soup into a blender and blend until smooth, return it to the rest of the soup in the pan and stir well. Reheat before serving and garnish each bowl with chopped parsley.

DIPS AND SNACKS

Savoury dips are often served with tortilla or plantain chips as little appetisers before the main course. Dips can also be simply spooned onto warmed tortillas or crusty bread rolls to eat as a snack. As well as being enjoyed as a dip, guacamole is another basic, which is regularly used as a topping or an accompaniment for a host of other dishes. Nachos, spiced peanuts and pumpkin seeds are useful little nibbles to serve with drinks, and along with the dips and 'chips', tortas and savoury baked rolls they make excellent buffet foods.

Guacamole (serves 4)

2 avocados, peeled and mashed

2 tomatoes, skinned and finely chopped

1 dessertspoon lemon or lime juice

1 rounded tablespoon finely chopped fresh coriander

2 spring onions, trimmed and finely chopped

½ green chilli, finely chopped

black pepper

Mix all ingredients together until well combined.

Savoury mince and tomato dip (serves 4)

¼ quantity savoury soya mince (see page 23)

¼ quantity tomato sauce (see page 41)

Blend the soya mince with the tomato sauce, adding a little water if necessary if the mixture is too thick. Put in a saucepan and heat gently until hot. Transfer to a serving dish and serve hot or cold.

Mushroom and bean dip (serves 4)

6oz/175g mushrooms, wiped and finely chopped

½ quantity refried beans (see page 22)

1 garlic clove, crushed

1 tablespoon corn oil

Heat the oil and gently fry the garlic and mushrooms until the juices run. Remove from the heat and add the refried beans and if necessary a little water to make a dipping consistency. Cover and chill until cold.

Layered dip

(serves 6)

½ quantity refried beans (see page 22)

1 quantity guacamole (see page 36)

½ quantity raw tomato sauce (see page 41)

4 spring onions, trimmed and finely sliced

finely chopped fresh coriander leaves

Thin the refried beans with a little water, if necessary, to get a thick dipping consistency and spoon onto a serving plate. Top with the guacamole and then the raw tomato sauce and sprinkle with spring onions and coriander.

Tortilla chips

(serves 4)

6 4 inch/10cm corn tortillas (see page 20)

corn oil

salt (optional)

Cut each tortilla into 6 triangle shapes. Deep fry in hot oil for a few minutes until golden brown. Drain on kitchen paper and sprinkle with salt if required.

Fried plantain chips

(serves 6)

2 green plantains

corn oil

salt (optional)

Peel and thinly slice the plantains, then deep fry the slices in hot oil until golden and crisp. Drain on kitchen paper and sprinkle with salt if wished.

Nachos

tortilla chips (see page 37)

grated meltable vegan 'cheese'

chopped bottled chillis

Spread the tortilla chips on a baking sheet. Sprinkle with grated 'cheese' and chopped chillis and place under a hot grill until the 'cheese' melts.

Roasted spiced peanuts and pumpkin seeds

(serves 4/6)

4oz/100g blanched peanuts, halved

4oz/100g pumpkin seeds

1 dessertspoon corn oil

½ teaspoon cayenne pepper

½ teaspoon ground cumin

black pepper

Heat the oil and add the peanuts, pumpkin seeds, cayenne pepper and cumin. Season with black pepper and stir well. Fry for about 5 minutes until just golden. Keep the nuts and seeds moving in the pan to prevent burning.

Savoury baked rolls

crusty rolls

refried beans (see page 22)

vegan margarine

grated vegan 'cheese'

finely chopped spring onions

Slice each roll in half and spread with margarine. Fill the rolls with refried beans and some finely chopped spring onions and grated 'cheese'. Replace the tops and bake in a preheated oven at 170°C/325°F/Gas mark 3 for 15 minutes. Serve with a salad garnish.

Tortas   *(serves 4/6)*

> 1 French stick, cut into 4 or 6 equal lengths
> refried beans (see page 22)
> guacamole (see page 36)
> shredded lettuce
> red onion rings
> sliced tomatoes
> grated vegan 'cheese'
> finely chopped green chillis

Cut each piece of French bread in half lengthwise and remove a little of the bread in the centre to accommodate the filling. Spread each half with refried beans, and add a little shredded lettuce, some onion rings and tomato slices and then a little guacamole on the bottom halves. Sprinkle with grated 'cheese' and some finely chopped chillis and replace the top halves.

SAUCES AND SALSAS

Sauces can form an integral part of a dish or be simply spooned over plainly cooked foods to liven them up and give them a Mexican flavour. Whichever way you use them, the sauces included here will be used regularly and, apart from the raw tomato sauce which needs to be freshly made, they can be frozen successfully. Some dishes only require small amounts of sauce, so it's a good idea to freeze them in small portions.

Salsas, which are sweet and savoury little uncooked mixtures made from finely chopped fruits and vegetables, are never absent from the Mexican spread. They are easy to prepare and make colourful and delicious accompaniments for snacks, light meals and main courses and they are also often stirred into bowls of soup at the table.

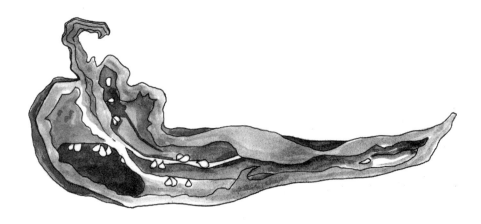

Tomato sauce

14oz/400g tin crushed tomatoes

1 medium onion, peeled and finely chopped

1 garlic clove, crushed

¼ red chilli, finely chopped

1 dessertspoon corn oil

1 dessertspoon tomato purée

½ teaspoon dried oregano

black pepper

Heat the oil and soften the onion, garlic and chilli. Add the remaining ingredients and stir well. Bring to the boil, cover and simmer gently for 10 minutes, stirring occasionally.

Raw tomato sauce

1lb/450g ripe tomatoes, skinned and finely chopped

2 spring onions, trimmed and finely chopped

1 garlic clove, crushed

1 dessertspoon finely chopped bottled red chilli

1 rounded tablespoon finely chopped fresh coriander

1 dessertspoon lime juice

1 dessertspoon olive oil

black pepper

Mix the ingredients until well combined and chill before use.

Chilli sauce

4 red chillis, finely chopped

12oz/350g ripe tomatoes, skinned and chopped

2 garlic cloves, crushed

1 small red onion, peeled and finely chopped

1 dessertspoon olive oil

1 dessertspoon lime juice

1 teaspoon demerara sugar

½ teaspoon ground cumin

black pepper

Heat the oil and gently fry the chillis, onion and garlic. Add the remaining ingredients and cook until the tomatoes are pulpy. Blend the mixture smooth, then return to the pan and reheat.

Mole sauce

14oz/400g tin crushed tomatoes

2oz/50g ground almonds

2oz/50g ground peanuts

1oz/25g raisins

1oz/25g sesame seeds

1oz/25g vegan chocolate, grated

1 onion, peeled and finely chopped

2 garlic cloves, crushed

2 red chillis, finely chopped

1 corn tortilla, shredded

2 tablespoons corn oil

½ teaspoon ground cinnamon

½ teaspoon fennel seeds

4 black peppercorns

5 fl.oz/150ml vegetable stock

Heat the oil in a large pan and fry the onion, garlic and chilli until soft. Add the almonds, peanuts, raisins, sesame seeds, cinnamon, fennel seeds and peppercorns and cook for 5 minutes while stirring. Remove from the heat and add the tortilla and tomatoes, then return to the heat and cook for 10 minutes, stirring frequently. Transfer to a blender and add the stock. Blend until smooth, return to the pan and add the chocolate. Stir over a low heat for about 5 minutes until the chocolate melts and combines with the sauce.

Mango and lime salsa   *(serves 4/6)*

12oz/350g mango flesh, finely chopped

4oz/100g tomato, skinned and finely chopped

½ small red onion, peeled and finely chopped

1 bottled red chilli, finely chopped

1 rounded tablespoon finely grated lime peel

1 rounded tablespoon finely chopped fresh coriander

1 dessertspoon lime juice

1 dessertspoon white wine vinegar

1 dessertspoon olive oil

Put the mango, tomato, onion, chilli, lime peel and coriander in a large bowl. Combine the lime juice with the vinegar and oil and add. Mix thoroughly, then transfer to a serving bowl and cover and chill before serving.

Sweetcorn salsa   *(serves 4/6)*

8oz/225g tinned sweetcorn kernels, drained

2oz/50g red pepper, finely chopped

2oz/50g orange pepper, finely chopped

2oz/50g tomato, skinned and finely chopped

1 small red onion, peeled and finely chopped

1 garlic clove, crushed

1 dessertspoon finely chopped bottled chilli

1 dessertspoon corn oil

1 dessertspoon lemon juice

2 dessertspoons white wine vinegar

1 teaspoon dried parsley

black pepper

Mash the sweetcorn kernels with a potato masher, put them in a bowl with the red and orange pepper, tomato, onion, garlic and chilli and combine well. Mix the corn oil with the lemon juice, vinegar and parsley, season with black pepper and spoon over the salsa. Stir very well and transfer to a serving bowl. Cover and chill.

Avocado, mushroom and tomato salsa   (serves 4/6)

1 large ripe avocado, peeled and finely chopped

4oz/100g mushrooms, wiped and finely chopped

4oz/100g ripe tomato, skinned and finely chopped

1 tablespoon chopped capers

1 dessertspoon olive oil

1 dessertspoon lemon juice

2 dessertspoons white wine vinegar

few drops tabasco sauce

pinch of ground bay leaves

black pepper

Mix the avocado with the mushrooms, tomato and capers. Combine the remaining ingredients and add. Mix thoroughly and spoon into a serving bowl. Cover and chill.

Roasted sweet pepper salsa   *(serves 4/6)*

4oz/100g red peppers

4oz/100g yellow peppers

4oz/100g green peppers

4oz/100g tomato, skinned and finely chopped

4 spring onions, peeled and finely chopped

1 garlic clove, crushed

1 small green chilli, finely chopped

1 dessertspoon chopped capers

1 rounded tablespoon finely chopped fresh parsley

1 dessertspoon olive oil

1 dessertspoon white wine vinegar

1 dessertspoon lime juice

black pepper

Put the peppers on a baking tray and place them under a hot grill, turning occasionally, until the skin blisters. Carefully peel off the skins and discard together with the stalks, membranes and seeds. Chop the pepper flesh finely and put it in a mixing bowl with the tomato, spring onions, garlic, chilli, capers and parsley. Mix the olive oil with the vinegar and lime juice, season with black pepper and spoon over the salsa. Combine well, transfer to a serving bowl, cover and chill.

Green salsa   *(serves 4/6)*

6oz/175g cucumber

4oz/100g green pepper

2oz/50g green olives

1 tablespoon capers

4 spring onions, trimmed

1 green chilli

2 rounded tablespoons finely chopped fresh coriander

black pepper

1 dessertspoon olive oil

1 dessertspoon white wine vinegar

1 dessertspoon lime juice

Finely chop the cucumber, pepper, olives, capers, spring onions and chilli and put them in a bowl. Combine the olive oil with the vinegar and lime juice and add to the salsa together with the coriander. Season with black pepper and mix thoroughly. Transfer to a serving bowl, cover and chill.

Pineapple salsa *(serves 4/6)*

12oz/350g pineapple flesh, finely chopped

2oz/50g green pepper, finely chopped

2oz/50g red pepper, finely chopped

4 spring onions, trimmed and finely chopped

1 tablespoon finely chopped bottled chilli

1 rounded tablespoon finely chopped fresh coriander

1 dessertspoon corn oil

1 dessertspoon lime juice

Drain any juice from the pineapple, then put the flesh in a mixing bowl with the peppers, onions, chilli and coriander. Combine the corn oil and the lime juice and spoon over the salsa. Mix well, transfer to a serving bowl, cover and chill.

RICE

The Spanish Conquistadores introduced rice to Mexico in the early sixteenth century and it has been a staple food ever since. Rice, or arroz as it is called in Mexico, is eaten by many on a daily basis, either as a 'dry soup', a main course, an accompaniment or for dessert. It is often just cooked in the liquid left over from cooking beans or it can be done in a more elaborate way by adding vegetables, beans and seasonings. A popular way of serving rice is to mould it into a ring and fill the centre with guacamole, salad or a savoury bean or vegetable mixture. To serve it in this way, simply spoon the cooked rice into an oiled ring mould, press it down firmly, invert the mould onto a serving plate and fill the centre.

White rice *(serves 4)*

8oz/225g long grain rice

1 onion, peeled and finely chopped

1 garlic clove, crushed

½ green chilli, finely chopped

1 tablespoon corn oil

20 fl.oz/600ml vegetable stock

Heat the oil and gently fry the onion, garlic and chilli until softened. Add the rice and fry for 1 minute more. Stir in the vegetable stock and bring to the boil. Cover and simmer gently until the liquid has been absorbed and the rice is done.

Vegetable rice *(serves 4)*

8oz/225g long grain rice

4oz/100g carrot, scraped and finely chopped

4oz/100g sweetcorn kernels

4oz/100g shelled peas

4oz/100g tomato, skinned and finely chopped

2oz/50g mushrooms, wiped and chopped

1 onion, peeled and finely chopped

2 garlic cloves, crushed

16 fl.oz/475ml vegetable stock

1 teaspoon dried oregano

½ teaspoon paprika

1 tablespoon corn oil

black pepper

chopped fresh parsley

Heat the oil and fry the onion and garlic until soft. Add the rice and stir around for 1 minute. Stir in the remaining ingredients apart from the parsley, and bring to the boil. Cover and simmer gently, until the liquid has been absorbed and the rice and vegetables are tender. Garnish with chopped parsley when serving.

Green rice *(serves 4)*

8oz/225g long grain rice

8oz/225g green pepper, finely chopped

1 onion, peeled and finely chopped

2 garlic cloves, crushed

1 small green chilli, finely chopped

4 rounded tablespoons fresh coriander

2 tablespoons corn oil

20 fl.oz/600ml vegetable stock

black pepper

chopped green olives

Gently soften the pepper, onion, garlic and chilli in the oil. Add the rice and stir around for another minute. Put the coriander and the stock in a blender, blend and add to the pan, then season with black pepper and bring to the boil. Cover and simmer until the liquid has been absorbed. Spoon the rice into a warmed serving dish and garnish with chopped green olives.

Tomato rice with peas (serves 4)

8oz/225g long grain rice

4oz/100g ripe tomato, skinned and finely chopped

4oz/100g shelled peas

1 red onion, peeled and finely chopped

1 small green chilli, finely chopped

2 garlic cloves, crushed

2 tablespoons corn oil

1 tablespoon tomato purée

16 fl.oz/475ml vegetable stock

black pepper

chopped fresh coriander leaves

cherry tomatoes

Heat the oil and gently fry the onion, chilli and garlic. Add the rice and stir around for 1 minute. Mash the 4oz/100g tomato and add to the pan, together with the peas, tomato purée and stock. Season with black pepper and stir well. Bring to the boil, cover and simmer gently until the liquid has been absorbed. Transfer the rice to a warmed serving dish and fork through. Garnish with fresh coriander and quartered cherry tomatoes.

Sweet pepper rice (serves 4)

8oz/225g long grain rice

8oz/225g mixed peppers (e.g. red, yellow, green and orange), chopped

2 garlic cloves, crushed

1 onion, peeled and finely chopped

1 tablespoon corn oil

20 fl.oz/600ml vegetable stock

1 rounded teaspoon cumin seed

few drops tabasco sauce

black pepper

pepper rings

fresh parsley sprigs

Heat the oil and gently fry the peppers, onion and garlic for 5 minutes. Add the cumin seed and rice and stir around for 1 minute more. Stir in the stock and tabasco sauce and season with black pepper. Bring to the boil, then cover and simmer gently until the liquid has been absorbed. Spoon the rice into a warmed serving dish and garnish with pepper rings and fresh parsley sprigs.

Mushroom and black bean rice   *(serves 4)*

8oz/225g long grain rice

8oz/225g mushrooms, wiped and chopped

4oz/100g cooked black beans

1 onion, peeled and finely chopped

1 garlic clove, crushed

1 tablespoon corn oil

1 tablespoon finely chopped fresh oregano

black pepper

20 fl.oz/600ml vegetable stock or cooking liquid from black beans

Soften the onion and garlic in the oil. Stir in the mushrooms and fry until the juices begin to run. Now add the rice and stir around for 1 minute. Add the remaining ingredients and stir well. Bring to the boil, cover and simmer gently until the liquid has been absorbed and the rice is cooked.

Avocado rice ring   *(serves 4)*

8oz/225g long grain rice

1 small avocado

20 fl.oz/600ml vegetable stock

1 tablespoon olive oil

1 dessertspoon lime juice

1 teaspoon marjoram

¼ teaspoon ground bay leaves

black pepper

lime slices

Peel the avocado and mash it with the lime juice. Heat the oil and gently fry the rice for 1 minute. Add the avocado, stock, marjoram and ground bay leaves, season with black pepper and stir well. Bring to the boil, cover and simmer very gently until the liquid has been absorbed. Spoon the rice into an oiled ring mould, press it down evenly, cover and refrigerate for a few hours until cold. Run a sharp knife around the edges of the mould and then invert the rice ring onto a serving plate. Garnish with lime slices and serve.

LIGHT MEALS

As the main Mexican meal of the day tends to be on the heavy side, the other meals are usually lighter and lots of these revolve around the tortilla in its many guises. Many of these dishes can be quickly put together if you have a supply of tortillas and other basics in the freezer. Light meals, or antojitos, are usually served with salad garnishes and salsa. All of the recipes in this section can also be used as starters and many of them make ideal buffet foods.

Savoury soya mince burritos with guacamole

(serves 4)

4 wheat tortillas (see page 21)
¼ quantity savoury soya mince (see page 23)
4 rounded tablespoons guacamole (see page 36)

Wrap the tortillas in foil and put them in a preheated oven at 180°C/350°F/Gas mark 4 for 5 minutes to soften. Divide the savoury soya mince between the warmed tortillas and fold each one up to make little square parcels. Place the parcels with the folds underneath in a greased baking dish, cover and return to the oven for 20 minutes. Spoon a tablespoonful of guacamole on top of each burrito when serving.

Enfrijoladas

(serves 4)

8 4 inch/10cm corn tortillas (see page 20)
½ quantity refried beans (see page 22)
½ quantity tomato sauce (see page 41)
2oz/50g vegan 'cheese', grated
1 red chilli, finely chopped
4 spring onions, trimmed and finely chopped
toasted pine kernels
corn oil

Heat a little corn oil and fry each tortilla for a few seconds. Drain on kitchen paper and keep warm. Put the tomato sauce in a small saucepan, bring to the boil and simmer uncovered for 5 minutes. Reheat the refried beans and spread evenly over the warm tortillas. Spoon the tomato sauce on top and sprinkle with the grated 'cheese', chilli, spring onions and pine kernels.

Tostadas   *(serves 4)*

> 8 4 inch/10cm corn tortillas (see page 20)
>
> ½ quantity refried beans (see page 22)
>
> corn oil
>
> 2 tomatoes, thinly sliced
>
> 1 avocado
>
> lemon or lime juice
>
> 6 spring onions, trimmed and finely sliced
>
> 2oz/50g vegan 'cheese', grated
>
> shredded lettuce
>
> 8 green olives, chopped
>
> chopped pecans

Peel and thinly slice the avocado and sprinkle the slices with lemon or lime juice. Fry each tortilla for a few seconds in a little corn oil. Drain them on kitchen paper and spread with the refried beans. Add a little shredded lettuce and tomato slices. Spread the grated 'cheese' on top and sprinkle with the spring onions, olives and pecans. Finish each tostada with some avocado slices.

Quesadillas   *(serves 4)*

> 4 wheat tortillas (see page 21)
>
> 8oz/225g tomato, skinned and finely chopped
>
> 2oz/50g vegan 'cheese', grated
>
> 1 small red onion, peeled and finely chopped
>
> small sprig of fresh thyme, chopped
>
> black pepper
>
> corn oil
>
> sesame seeds

Wrap the tortillas in foil and put them in a preheated oven at 180°C/350°F/Gas mark 4 for 5 minutes to soften. Mix the tomato with the onion and thyme and divide this between the tortillas, placing it on one half of each circle only. Sprinkle the grated 'cheese' over the filling and season with black pepper. Fold the tortillas over to enclose the filling and place them in a greased baking dish. Brush the tops with corn oil and sprinkle with sesame seeds. Return to the oven for about 15 minutes until golden brown.

Enchiladas with onion mole *(serves 4)*

> 4 wheat tortillas (see page 21)
> ¼ quantity mole sauce (see page 42)
> 1 large red onion, peeled
> 1 dessertspoon corn oil
> extra corn oil
> sesame seeds

Cut a few onion rings and keep for garnish. Finely chop the rest of the onion and fry in the dessertspoonful of oil until softened. Heat a small amount of oil in a frying pan and briefly fry the tortillas. Thin the mole sauce with a little water if necessary to make a coating consistency. Dip each tortilla in the sauce, divide the onion between them and roll them up. Put them in a greased baking dish and spoon any remaining sauce on top. Sprinkle with sesame seeds and cover. Bake in a preheated oven at 180°C/350°F/Gas mark 4 for 15 minutes. Serve garnished with the onion rings.

Fried bean flautas *(serves 4)*

> 4 wheat tortillas (see page 21)
> ½ quantity refried beans (see page 22)
> ½ quantity tomato sauce (see page 41)

corn oil

grated vegan 'cheese'

chopped fresh coriander leaves

Wrap the tortillas in foil and put them in a preheated oven at 180°C/350°F/Gas mark 4 for 5 minutes to soften. Warm the refried beans and divide between the tortillas, spreading it evenly. Roll the tortillas up and shallow fry them in hot corn oil until browned. Drain on kitchen paper. Heat the tomato sauce and spoon some on top of each flauta. Garnish with grated 'cheese' and chopped coriander.

Mushroom and tomato sincronizadas   *(serves 4)*

4 wheat tortillas (see page 21)

4oz/100g mushrooms, wiped and chopped

2 garlic cloves, crushed

1 dessertspoon olive oil

1oz/25g vegan 'cheese', grated

½ quantity raw tomato sauce (see page 41)

vegan margarine

Fry the mushrooms and garlic in the olive oil until the juices begin to run. Lightly grease a 7 inch/18cm non-stick frying pan with margarine and put one of the tortillas in the pan. Spread half of the mushrooms on the tortilla, then half of the 'cheese', and finally half of the tomato sauce. Place another tortilla on top and cook for a few minutes whilst pressing down lightly with a serving slice. Carefully invert the sincronizada onto a plate, then slide it into the pan with the cooked side up. Cook the underside for a few minutes, slide it back onto the plate and cut into wedges with a sharp knife. Repeat with the remaining tortillas and filling.

Vegetable and kidney bean tacos   *(serves 4)*

4 taco shells

filling

4oz/100g ripe tomato, skinned and chopped

2oz/50g red pepper, finely chopped

2oz/50g yellow pepper, finely chopped

1 small onion, peeled and finely chopped

2 garlic cloves, crushed

1 green chilli, finely chopped

½oz/15g natural minced textured vegetable protein

2oz/50g cooked red kidney beans

1 dessertspoon corn oil

1 dessertspoon tomato purée

2 fl.oz/50ml vegetable stock or water

1 tablespoon finely chopped fresh parsley

black pepper

shredded lettuce

grated vegan 'cheese'

Heat the oil and fry the onion, garlic and chilli until soft. Add the tomato, red and yellow pepper, vegetable protein, tomato purée, stock and parsley. Season with black pepper and stir well. Bring to the boil, cover and simmer gently for 10 minutes, stirring occasionally. Add the kidney beans and continue cooking for another 5 minutes, until the mixture is thick. Warm the tacos and put a little shredded lettuce in each one. Divide the filling between them and sprinkle the tops with grated 'cheese'.

Broccoli and mushroom fajitas   *(serves 4)*

4 wheat tortillas (see page 21)

8oz/225g broccoli, chopped

4oz/100g mushrooms, wiped and finely chopped

1 onion, peeled and finely chopped

1 garlic clove, crushed

1 green chilli, finely chopped

1 dessertspoon corn oil

4 fl.oz/125ml vegetable stock

4 fl.oz/125ml soya milk

2 tablespoons finely chopped fresh coriander

1 dessertspoon cornflour

black pepper

shredded lettuce

chopped pecans

lime wedges

Soften the onion, garlic and chilli in the oil. Put in the mushrooms and fry until the juices begin to run. Add the broccoli, stock and coriander and season with black pepper, stir well and simmer gently until the vegetables are just tender. Meanwhile, wrap the tortillas in foil and place them in a preheated oven at 180°C/350°F/Gas mark 4 for 5 minutes to soften. Mix the cornflour with the soya milk until smooth, add to the pan and stir well. Bring back to the boil whilst stirring and simmer for a minute or two until the sauce thickens. Arrange a little shredded lettuce along the centre of each warm tortilla. Divide the broccoli mixture evenly between the tortillas, spooning it carefully on top of the lettuce, and roll each tortilla up into a cone shape enclosing the filling. Serve garnished with lime wedges.

Tamales   *(serves 6)*

Tamales are traditionally steamed in the husks from corn cobs, tied with thin lengths of corn 'string'. If you want to cook tamales in this way the husks need to be soaked in boiling water for about an hour to soften them.

> 10oz/300g masa harina
>
> 4oz/100g vegan margarine
>
> 6 fl.oz/175ml vegetable stock
>
> 1 teaspoon baking powder
>
> pinch of salt
>
> ¼ quantity savoury soya mince (see page 23)
>
> extra vegan margarine
>
> 1 quantity chilli sauce (see page 42)

Cream the 4oz/100g margarine in a mixing bowl. Mix the baking powder and salt with the masa harina and gradually work into the margarine, alternating with the stock. Mix well until a soft dough forms. Cut 6 pieces of cooking foil measuring 10 inches/25cm square. Lightly grease the centre of each square with margarine and divide the dough equally between them, shaping it into an oblong of about 5½ x 4½ inches/14 x 11.5cm. Divide the savoury soya mince between the oblongs, spreading it along the middle between the two shorter sides. Loosen the dough on one side and fold over the filling. Fold the other side over while wrapping the whole parcel in the foil. Put the parcels in a steamer and steam for 1½ hours, keeping the boiling water topped up regularly. Carefully unwrap the tamales and serve hot with chilli sauce.

Sweetcorn and pepper flan — (*serves 4*)

base

4oz/100g sweetcorn kernels

4oz/100g plain flour

2oz/50g vegan margarine

1 rounded teaspoon baking powder

filling

4oz/100g sweetcorn kernels, blanched

4oz/100g red pepper, finely chopped

4oz/100g orange pepper, finely chopped

1 red onion, peeled and finely chopped

1 garlic clove, crushed

1 green chilli, finely chopped

1 tablespoon corn oil

¼ quantity tomato sauce (see page 41)

grated vegan 'cheese'

Cook the sweetcorn kernels for the base until tender, then drain and mash with a potato masher. Add the margarine and place over a low heat until it melts. Remove from the heat and add the sifted flour and baking powder and mix very well. Turn out onto a floured board and roll out to fit a lined and greased 8 inch/20cm round loose-bottomed flan tin. Prick the base with a fork and bake in a preheated oven at 180°C/350°F/Gas mark 4 for 5 minutes.

Heat the oil and gently fry the peppers, onion, garlic and chilli for 10 minutes. Remove from the heat and add the drained sweetcorn and the tomato sauce. Mix well and spoon the filling evenly into the flan case. Return to the oven and bake for 30 minutes. Garnish with grated 'cheese' and cut into 4 wedges when serving.

Aubergine mole tarts

(serves 4/6)

bases

6oz/175g cornmeal

3oz/75g plain flour

pinch of salt

1 teaspoon baking powder

approx. 6 fl.oz/175ml warm water

corn oil

filling

9oz/250g aubergine, finely chopped

1 onion, peeled and finely chopped

2 tablespoons corn oil

¼ quantity mole sauce (see page 42)

toasted sesame seeds

Mix the cornmeal, flour, salt and baking powder in a large bowl. Gradually add the warm water until everything binds together. Divide the mixture into 18 equal pieces and roll each piece into a ball. Roll the balls lightly in flour and shape them into little tart cases. Deep fry these in hot corn oil for a few minutes until golden, then drain on kitchen paper and keep warm while making the filling.

Heat the 2 tablespoonfuls of oil in a pan and gently fry the aubergine and onion for about 15 minutes until soft. Add the mole sauce and mix thoroughly. Simmer for a couple of minutes until heated through, adding a little water if the mixture is too thick. Spoon the filling into the tart cases and sprinkle the tops with sesame seeds.

Empanadas

(serves 6)

pastry

8oz/225g plain flour

4oz/100g vegan margarine

water

soya milk

sesame seeds

filling

6oz/175g courgette, finely chopped

4oz/100g tomato, skinned and chopped

2oz/50g sweetcorn kernels

1 medium red onion, peeled and finely chopped

1 garlic clove, crushed

1 red chilli, finely chopped

1 dessertspoon corn oil

1 dessertspoon tomato purée

1 tablespoon finely chopped fresh coriander leaves

black pepper

Rub the margarine into the flour and add enough water to make a soft dough. Knead well then chill for an hour.

Heat the oil and soften the onion, garlic and chilli. Add the remaining filling ingredients and stir well. Cook gently until the courgette is soft and the mixture thickens, stirring occasionally to prevent sticking. Remove from the heat and allow to cool.

Knead the dough again and divide it into 6 equal portions. Roll each portion out on a floured board into a 5½ inch/14cm circle. Divide the filling between the circles, placing it on one side only. Dampen the edges with water and fold the pastry over to enclose the filling. Press the edges together to join and transfer the empanadas to a greased baking sheet. Make three slits in the top of each one with a sharp knife. Brush the tops with soya milk and sprinkle with sesame seeds. Bake in a preheated oven at 180°C/350°F/Gas mark 4 for 25-30 minutes until golden.

Cauliflower and courgette gratins (serves 4)

8oz/225g cauliflower, cut into florets

8oz/225g courgette, sliced

2oz/50g mushrooms, wiped and chopped

1 dessertspoon olive oil

1 quantity tomato sauce (see page 41)

topping

1oz/25g breadcrumbs

1oz/25g vegan 'cheese', grated

Heat the oil and gently fry the mushrooms until the juices begin to run. Add the tomato sauce and leave to simmer while cooking the vegetables. Steam the cauliflower and courgette until just tender, then divide between 4 individual warm ovenproof dishes. Pour the hot sauce over the vegetables, mix the breadcrumbs with the grated 'cheese' and spread over the top. Place under a hot grill for a few minutes until browned.

Avocado and pepper cocktail (serves 4)

2 medium avocados

1 red pepper

1 green pepper

1 yellow pepper

1 orange pepper

4oz/100g tomato, skinned and finely chopped

1 garlic clove, crushed

1 bottled chilli, finely chopped

black pepper

1 dessertspoon olive oil

1 tablespoon white wine vinegar

shredded crisp lettuce leaves

cucumber slices, halved

toasted pine kernels

chopped fresh parsley

Place the peppers under a hot grill until the skins blister, turning frequently to avoid burning. Allow to cool slightly, then peel off the skins and chop the peppers. Peel, stone and chop the avocados and put them in a mixing bowl with the peppers. Mix the olive oil with the vinegar, add the tomato, garlic and chilli and season with black pepper. Add to the peppers and avocado and toss thoroughly. Arrange some shredded lettuce in 4 serving dishes. Spoon the salad mixture on top of the lettuce, garnish with halved cucumber slices and sprinkle with pine kernels and chopped parsley.

Courgette and pumpkin seed pudding   *(serves 4/6)*

8oz/225g courgette, grated

2oz/50g pumpkin seeds, ground

2oz/50g breadcrumbs

2oz/50g masa harina

1 onion, peeled and finely chopped

1 garlic clove, crushed

1 dessertspoon corn oil

1 teaspoon dried oregano

pinch of ground bay leaves

black pepper

4 fl.oz/125ml soya milk

extra pumpkin seeds

Heat the oil and gently fry the onion and garlic until soft. Remove from the heat and add the courgette, ground pumpkin seeds, breadcrumbs, masa harina, oregano and ground bay leaves. Season with black pepper and mix well. Add the soya milk and combine thoroughly. Spoon the mixture into a greased 8 inch/20cm diameter loose-bottomed flan tin. Sprinkle the top with pumpkin seeds and press these in lightly with the back of a spoon. Bake in a preheated oven at 180°C/350°F/Gas mark 4 for about 35 minutes until golden brown. Cut into wedges to serve.

Savoury corn cakes (serves 4/6)

8oz/225g sweetcorn kernels

6oz/175g masa harina

2oz/50g plain flour

1oz/50g vegan margarine

1 onion, peeled and finely chopped

1 garlic clove, crushed

1 green chilli, finely chopped

5 fl.oz/150ml soya milk

1 dessertspoon corn oil

1 teaspooon dried parsley

black pepper

extra corn oil

Blanch the sweetcorn kernels and drain. Heat the dessertspoonful of oil and fry the onion, garlic and chilli until softened. Add the margarine and stir until it melts, then remove from the heat and stir in half of the sweetcorn kernels and the parsley. Blend the remaining sweetcorn with the soya milk, add to the pan and stir well. Gradually work in the masa harina and flour and then season with black pepper. Mix thoroughly, cover and chill for a couple of hours. Take rounded tablespoonfuls of the mixture and shape them into flat rounds of about ½ inch/1cm thick. Shallow fry in hot oil for a few minutes on each side until golden. Drain on kitchen paper and serve warm.

Courgette and pecan croquetas   (*serves 4*)

8oz/225g courgette, grated

3oz/75g pecans, ground

1 onion, peeled and finely chopped

1 garlic clove, crushed

1 green chilli, finely chopped

2oz/50g breadcrumbs

2oz/50g plain flour

2 tablespoons finely chopped fresh coriander leaves

1 rounded teaspoon ground cumin

black pepper

1 tablespoon corn oil

extra corn oil

Heat the tablespoonful of oil and gently fry the onion, garlic and chilli until soft. Remove from the heat and add the remaining ingredients, mixing thoroughly. Divide the mixture into 8 equal portions and shape each one into a croquette. Put these on a plate, cover and keep in the fridge for an hour. Shallow fry the croquetas in hot oil, turning to ensure even cooking, until golden brown. Drain on kitchen paper and serve warm.

Baked stuffed avocado   (*serves 4*)

2 avocados, halved and stoned

filling

2oz/50g vegan 'cream cheese'

2oz/50g mushrooms, wiped and finely chopped

1oz/25g pecans, grated

1 dessertspoon olive oil

1 teaspoon parsley

black pepper

Heat the oil and fry the mushrooms until the juices begin to run. Remove from the heat and add the remaining filling ingredients. Mix well and divide the filling between the hollows of the avocado halves, shaping it into round mounds on top. Put the avocados in a greased baking dish and bake in a preheated oven at 180°C/350°F/Gas mark 4 for 20 minutes.

Stuffed baked chayote
(serves 4)

> 2 chayotes
>
> 4oz/100g vegan 'cream cheese'
>
> 2oz/50g tomato, skinned and finely chopped
>
> 1oz/25g walnuts, grated
>
> 2 spring onions, trimmed and finely chopped
>
> 1 garlic clove, crushed
>
> 1 dessertspoon finely chopped bottled chilli
>
> black pepper
>
> 1oz/25g breadcrumbs

Wash the chayotes and put them in a saucepan. Cover with water, bring to the boil and simmer for 30-40 minutes until just tender. Meanwhile, make the filling. Mix the 'cream cheese' with the tomato, walnuts, onions, garlic and chilli and season with black pepper.

Halve the chayotes lengthwise and remove the seeds. Scoop out some of the flesh from the centre of each chayote half, mash this and mix it with the filling. Spoon the mixture into the hollows of the chayote halves, place them in a greased baking dish and sprinkle the breadcrumbs on top. Bake in a preheated oven at 180°C/350°F/Gas mark 4 for 15-20 minutes until golden.

MAIN COURSES

In Mexico the platos fuertes *is just one of several substantial courses served at the main meal of the day. For more modest appetites one of the following dishes with the suggested accompaniment will provide a filling meal with a Mexican flavour.*

Vegetable chilli with wild rice   *(serves 4)*

8oz/225g mixed long grain brown and wild rice

4oz/100g sweetcorn kernels

chopped fresh coriander leaves

chopped pecans

sauce

1lb/450g ripe tomatoes, skinned and chopped

8oz/225g carrot, scraped and grated

8oz/225g button mushrooms, wiped and halved

8oz/225g cooked red kidney beans

6oz/175g red pepper, chopped

6oz/175g green pepper, chopped

2oz/50g natural minced textured vegetable protein

1 red onion, peeled and finely chopped

2 celery sticks, trimmed and finely sliced

2 garlic cloves, crushed

2 green chillis, finely chopped

10 fl.oz/300ml vegetable stock

2 tablespoons finely chopped fresh coriander

2 tablespoons corn oil

1 tablespoon tomato purée

1 dessertspoon tamarind purée

2 bay leaves

1 teaspoon paprika

½-1 teaspoon ground chilli powder

¼ teaspoon ground cinnamon

black pepper

Heat the oil in a large pan and gently fry the onion, celery, garlic and chillis until softened. Add the tomato and cook until pulpy. Now add the remaining sauce ingredients and stir well. Bring to the boil and simmer gently for 15-20 minutes, until the vegetables are tender and the sauce thickens. Stir frequently to prevent sticking, adding a little more stock or water if necessary.

While the sauce is simmering cook the rice with the sweetcorn kernels and drain. Garnish the sauce with chopped coriander and pecans and serve with the rice, a green salad and warmed wheat tortillas.

Cornmeal and vegetable pie *(serves 4)*

8oz/225g cornmeal

40 fl.oz/1200ml water

½ teaspoon cayenne pepper

1 dessertspoon chives

filling

6oz/175g tomato, skinned and chopped

4oz/100g broccoli, chopped

4oz/100g carrot, scraped and chopped

4oz/100g red pepper, chopped

3oz/75g shelled broad beans

3oz/75g cooked borlotti beans

1oz/25g natural minced textured vegetable protein

1 red onion, peeled and finely chopped

2 garlic cloves, crushed

1 red chilli, finely chopped

1 tablespoon corn oil

6 fl.oz/175ml vegetable stock

½ teaspoon paprika

1 rounded teaspoon dried parsley

1 bay leaf

black pepper

Soften the onion, garlic and chilli in the oil. Add the tomato and cook until pulpy. Stir in the remaining filling ingredients and bring to the boil. Cover and simmer for 10 minutes, stirring occasionally.

Bring the water to the boil in a large pan. Mix the cayenne pepper and chives with the cornmeal. Take the water off the heat and gradually add the cornmeal, whisking well before adding more to avoid lumps. Return to a low heat and cook for 10-15 minutes, whilst stirring, until the cornmeal is thick and smooth. Spoon half of the mixture into a greased 10 x 8 inch/25 x 20cm deep casserole dish. Spread it out evenly, then top with the filling. Spread the remaining cornmeal mixture evenly on top and bake in a preheated oven at 180°C/350°F/Gas mark 4 for 40 minutes until golden. Serve with a vegetable dish or salad.

Stuffed baked courgettes   *(serves 4)*

4 courgettes, each approx. 8oz/225g

6oz/175g sweetcorn kernels, cooked and mashed

4oz/100g mushrooms, wiped and finely chopped

2oz/50g pecans, grated

1 medium onion, peeled and finely chopped

2 garlic cloves, crushed

1 green chilli, finely chopped

1 tablespoon corn oil

1 teaspoon dried thyme

black pepper

1 quantity tomato sauce (see page 41)

grated vegan 'cheese'

chopped fresh parsley

Top and tail the courgettes and cut in half lengthwise. Scoop out the centres, leaving shells of about ¼ inch/5mm thick. Finely chop the flesh.

Fry the onion, garlic and chilli in the oil until soft. Add the courgette flesh and the mushrooms and fry for 3 minutes. Remove from the heat and add the sweetcorn, pecans and thyme. Season with black pepper and mix thoroughly.

Fill the courgette shells with the mixture and put them in a greased shallow baking dish. Spoon the tomato sauce over the top, cover and bake in a preheated oven at 180°C/350°F/Gas mark 4 for 35-40 minutes until the courgettes are tender. Sprinkle with grated 'cheese' and garnish with chopped parsley. Serve with a savoury rice dish.

'Cheese' and vegetable chilaquiles   *(serves 4)*

8 4 inch/10cm corn tortillas (see page 20)

corn oil

2 chayotes, peeled and diced

8oz/225g sweetcorn kernels

8oz/225g green beans, topped, tailed and cut into 1 inch/2.5cm
    lengths

4oz/100g red pepper, chopped

4oz/100g orange pepper, chopped

3oz/75g vegan 'cheese', grated

1 onion, peeled and chopped

2 garlic cloves, crushed

1 dessertspoon corn oil

4 fl.oz/125ml vegetable stock

18 fl.oz/550ml soya milk

½oz/15g cornflour

1 rounded teaspoon dried oregano

1 bay leaf

black pepper

2oz/50g pecans, grated

1 rounded tablespoon vegan 'Parmesan'

chopped fresh parsley

Soften the onion and garlic in the dessertspoonful of oil in a large pan. Add the chayotes, red and orange peppers, sweetcorn, green beans, stock, oregano and bay leaf, season with black pepper and stir well. Bring to the boil, cover and simmer for about 10 minutes, stirring occasionally, until the vegetables are just done, then remove from the heat.

Cut the tortillas into thin strips and fry in hot corn oil until golden. Drain on kitchen paper and add to the vegetables. Dissolve the cornflour in the soya milk and add to the pan together with the grated 'cheese'. Stir well and bring to the boil whilst stirring. Continue stirring for a minute or two until the sauce thickens. Spoon into a greased baking dish and sprinkle the grated pecans and 'Parmesan' on top. Bake in a preheated oven at 180°C/350°F/Gas mark 4 for about 15 minutes until golden brown. Garnish with chopped parsley and serve with salad.

Aubergine and sweet potato casserole   (serves 4)

> 1¼lb/550g aubergine, diced
>
> 1¼lb/550g sweet potato, peeled and diced
>
> 1 quantity tomato sauce (see page 41)
>
> 8oz/225g red pepper, chopped
>
> 4oz/100g cooked red kidney beans
>
> 2oz/50g natural minced textured vegetable protein
>
> 1 red onion, peeled and finely chopped
>
> 2 green chillis, finely chopped
>
> 4 tablespoons corn oil
>
> 1 teaspoon ground cumin
>
> 16 fl.oz/475ml vegetable stock
>
> 1oz/25g tortilla chips (see page 37), crushed

Heat the oil and gently fry the aubergine, onion and chillis for 10 minutes, stirring frequently to prevent sticking. Add the tomato sauce, vegetable protein, red pepper, cumin and stock and combine well. Bring to the boil, cover and simmer for 10 minutes, stirring occasionally. Remove from the heat and stir in the kidney beans. Transfer the mixture to a greased shallow ovenproof dish. Put the sweet potato in a large pan of water and bring to the boil. Simmer for a few minutes until almost tender. Drain and arrange evenly over the aubergine mixture. Sprinkle the crushed tortilla chips on top, cover and bake in a preheated oven at 180°C/350°F/Gas mark 4 for 30 minutes. Serve with a green salad.

Stuffed baked peppers *(serves 4)*

> 4 peppers, each approx. 6oz/175g
> ½ quantity savoury soya mince (see page 23)
> ½ quantity tomato sauce (see page 41)
> grated vegan 'cheese'
> chopped fresh parsley

Put the peppers on a baking tray under a hot grill, turning them occasionally, until the skins blister. Carefully peel off the skins and cut out the stalks. Pull out the membranes and seeds and fill each pepper through the hole with the savoury soya mince. Place the filled peppers in a lightly oiled baking dish and spoon the tomato sauce on the tops. Cover and bake in a preheated oven at 180°C/350°F/Gas mark 4 for 30 minutes. Sprinkle the tops with grated 'cheese' and garnish with fresh parsley. Serve with a savoury rice dish.

Noodles with mixed vegetables *(serves 4)*

> 8oz/225g tomato, skinned and chopped
> 8oz/225g courgette, chopped
> 4oz/100g cooked red kidney beans
> 2oz/50g cauliflower, cut into small florets
> 2oz/50g sweetcorn kernels
> 2oz/50g button mushrooms, wiped and sliced
> 1 onion, peeled and finely chopped

2 garlic cloves, crushed

1 red chilli, finely chopped

3oz/75g thin noodles

18 fl.oz/550ml vegetable stock

1 tablespoon finely chopped fresh coriander

1 teaspoon ground coriander

½ teaspoon paprika

1 tablespoon tomato purée

1 dessertspoon corn oil

1 bay leaf

black pepper

1 avocado

lemon or lime juice

chopped pecans

Heat the oil in a large pan and fry the onion, garlic and chilli until soft. Add the tomato and cook until pulpy, then the courgette, cauliflower, sweetcorn, stock, fresh and ground coriander, paprika, tomato purée and bay leaf. Season with black pepper and stir well. Bring to the boil, cover and simmer for 10 minutes. Add the kidney beans, mushrooms and noodles and again stir well. Bring back to the boil and simmer gently for about 10 minutes, until the noodles are done and the mixture is thick. Peel and slice the avocado, sprinkle with lemon or lime juice and use as garnish together with some chopped pecans. Serve with warm cornbread and salad.

Peanut, lentil and squash stew (serves 4)

2lb/900g butternut squash

8oz/225g red lentils

8oz/225g tomato, skinned and chopped

4oz/100g roasted peanuts, ground

1 onion, peeled and chopped

2 garlic cloves, crushed

1 red chilli, finely chopped

1 dessertspoon corn oil

36 fl.oz/1075ml vegetable stock

2 rounded teaspoons ground cumin

1 teaspoon paprika

black pepper

chopped roasted peanuts, toasted

chopped fresh coriander leaves

Peel the butternut squash, remove the membranes and seeds and dice the flesh. Gently fry the onion, garlic and chilli in the oil in a large pan for 5 minutes. Add the tomato, cumin and paprika and cook until the tomato is pulpy. Stir in the stock and lentils and bring to the boil. Cover and simmer for 15 minutes. Add the diced squash and season with black pepper, then bring back to the boil, cover and simmer for 10 minutes, stirring occasionally. Toast the ground peanuts until golden and add to the pan. Stir well and continue simmering for about 5 minutes until the squash is tender and the mixture is thick. Stir frequently and add a little more stock or water if necessary to prevent sticking. Garnish with chopped toasted peanuts and fresh coriander and serve with a savoury rice dish.

Green vegetable and cornbread gratin   (serves 4)

12oz/350g shelled broad beans

12oz/350g courgette, chopped

12oz/350g leek, trimmed and finely sliced

8oz/225g green pepper, chopped

8oz/225g green beans, topped, tailed and cut into ½ inch/1cm lengths

2 garlic cloves, crushed

1 green chilli, finely chopped

1 medium avocado

1 tablespoon corn oil

2 tablespoons finely chopped fresh parsley

1 bay leaf

black pepper

1 dessertspoon lemon juice

1 rounded tablespoon cornflour

9 fl.oz/250ml vegetable stock

4 fl.oz/125ml soya milk

topping

8oz/225g cornbread (see page 111)

1 tablespoon vegan 'Parmesan'

Blanch the broad beans, then rinse under cold running water. Carefully remove the skins and discard. Heat the oil in a large pan and gently fry the leek, garlic and chilli for 5 minutes. Add the broad beans, courgette, green pepper and beans, parsley, bay leaf and stock. Season with black pepper and stir well. Bring to the boil, cover and simmer for 10 minutes, stirring occasionally. Mash the avocado with the lemon juice and add to the pan. Dissolve the cornflour in the soya milk and add as well. Stir thoroughly and bring to the boil. Continue stirring for a minute or two until the sauce thickens, then transfer the mixture to a greased shallow baking dish.

Crumble the cornbread into crumbs and mix with the 'Parmesan'. Sprinkle this topping evenly over the vegetables. Cover the dish and bake in a preheated oven at 180°C/350°F/Gas mark 4 for 15 minutes, then uncover and bake for another 5-10 minutes until golden brown. Serve with salad.

Spicy pecan balls in tomato sauce *(serves 4)*

4oz/100g pecans, ground

4oz/100g carrot, scraped and grated

4oz/100g plain flour

2oz/50g cornbread crumbs

2oz/50g natural minced textured vegetable protein

1 onion, peeled and grated

2 garlic cloves, crushed

10 fl.oz/300ml vegetable stock

1 tablespoon corn oil

1 rounded teaspoon ground cumin

1 teaspoon chilli powder

black pepper

1 tablespoon finely chopped fresh coriander

1 quantity tomato sauce (see page 41)

few drops tabasco sauce

extra corn oil

chopped fresh parsley

Fry the carrot, onion and garlic in the oil until softened. Add the vegetable protein, cumin, chilli powder, coriander and stock and stir well. Bring to the boil, then simmer gently for 10 minutes until the liquid has been absorbed, stirring frequently to prevent sticking. Remove from the heat and add the pecans, flour and cornbread crumbs, season with black pepper and mix thoroughly. Cover and chill for a couple of hours. Take rounded dessertspoonfuls of the mixture and shape into balls in the palm of the hand. Put these in an oiled ovenproof dish and brush them with corn oil. Bake in a preheated oven at 180°C/350°F/Gas mark 4 for 30 minutes.

About 10 minutes before the pecan balls are ready mix a few drops of tabasco with the tomato sauce and heat until hot. Take the nut balls out of the oven and pour the sauce over them. Garnish with fresh parsley and serve with a savoury rice dish.

Tortilla pie

(serves 4)

6 7 inch/18cm wheat tortillas (see page 21)

filling

14oz/400g tin crushed tomatoes

4oz/100g carrot, scraped and grated

4oz/100g mushrooms, wiped and chopped

4oz/100g leek, trimmed and finely sliced

4oz/100g red pepper, chopped

1 onion, peeled and finely chopped

2 garlic cloves, crushed

1 green chilli, finely chopped

2oz/50g natural minced textured vegetable protein

1 tablespoon corn oil

1 tablespoon finely chopped fresh coriander

1 dessertspoon tomato purée

1 bay leaf

black pepper

7 fl.oz/200ml vegetable stock

grated meltable vegan 'cheese'

chopped pecans

Fry the carrot, leek, red pepper, onion, garlic and chilli in the oil for 5 minutes. Add the vegetable protein, tomatoes, mushrooms, coriander, tomato purée, bay leaf and stock and season with black pepper. Stir well and bring to the boil, then cover and simmer, stirring occasionally, for 10 minutes.

Put a tortilla in a deep 7 inch/18cm greased casserole dish and cover with some of the filling. Repeat these layers with the other 5 tortillas. Sprinkle the top with grated 'cheese' and pecans. Cover and bake in a preheated oven at 180°C/350°F/Gas mark 4 for 35 minutes. Cut into 4 equal portions and serve with a savoury rice dish and salad.

Aubergine enchiladas with red pepper sauce

(serves 4)

8 7 inch/18cm wheat tortillas (see page 21)

corn oil

grated vegan 'cheese'

filling

1½lb/675g aubergine, finely chopped

4 garlic cloves, crushed

2 red chillis, finely chopped

1 large red onion, peeled and finely chopped

6 tablespoons corn oil

½ quantity tomato sauce (see page 41)

sauce

8oz/225g red pepper, finely chopped

1 red onion, peeled and finely chopped

2 garlic cloves, crushed

1 tablespoon corn oil

1 teaspoon dried oregano

few drops tabasco sauce

black pepper

4 fl.oz/125ml water

Heat the oil for the filling in a large pan and gently fry the aubergine, onion, garlic and chilli for 15 minutes, stirring frequently to prevent sticking. Add the tomato sauce and cook for a further 5 minutes, until the mixture has reduced down and the aubergine is tender.

Heat the oil for the sauce and soften the red pepper, onion and garlic for 5 minutes. Add the water, oregano and tabasco sauce and season with black pepper. Stir well and bring to the boil, then cover and simmer for 5 minutes. Transfer to a blender and blend until smooth.

Shallow fry the wheat tortillas in hot oil for about 30 seconds on each side. Drain on kitchen paper and keep them warm until they are all done. Divide the filling between the tortillas, placing it neatly along the centre. Roll the tortillas up to enclose the filling and put them with the joins underneath in a greased shallow baking dish. Spoon the sauce over the top and cover the dish. Bake in a preheated oven at 180°C/350°F/Gas mark 4 for 25 minutes. Garnish with grated 'cheese' and serve with a vegetable dish.

Mixed vegetable and bean hotpot *(serves 4)*

1lb/450g potatoes, peeled and diced

1lb/450g mixed peppers, chopped

12oz/350g courgette, chopped

8oz/225g cooked mixed beans

2oz/50g button mushrooms, wiped and halved

2 14oz/400g tins crushed tomatoes

1 onion, peeled and chopped

2 garlic cloves, crushed

14 fl.oz/400ml vegetable stock

1 tablespoon corn oil

1 tablespoon tomato purée

1 dessertspoon molasses

1 rounded teaspoon dried thyme

1 teaspoon chilli powder

1 teaspoon paprika

2 bay leaves

black pepper

grated vegan 'cheese'

finely chopped fresh parsley

Gently fry the onion and garlic in the oil in a large pan until soft. Add the potatoes and stock and bring to the boil, then cover and simmer for 10 minutes. Add the remaining ingredients except the beans, 'cheese' and parsley. Stir well and bring back to the boil. Cover and simmer for 15 minutes, then add the beans. Continue simmering for another 10-15 minutes until the vegetables are done, stirring occasionally to prevent sticking. Garnish with grated 'cheese' and parsley and serve with white rice (see page 48).

Baked tamales with tomato and pepper sauce

(serves 4)

> 1 quantity cooked tamales (see page 60)
> 1 quantity tomato sauce (see page 41)
> 1lb/450g mixed peppers, chopped
> 1 tablespoon corn oil
> 4 fl.oz/125ml vegetable stock
> 2oz/50g vegan 'cheese', grated
> chopped fresh coriander

Heat the oil and gently fry the peppers until softened. Add the tomato sauce and stock and simmer for 2 minutes. Chop the tamales into squares, put them in a greased baking dish and spoon the sauce evenly over the top. Cover and bake in a preheated oven at 180°C/350°F/Gas mark 4 for 20 minutes. Sprinkle the grated 'cheese' on top and garnish with chopped coriander. Serve with a vegetable dish or salad.

VEGETABLES

As well as the more elaborate vegetable dishes found here, lightly steamed vegetables served with Mexican-style sauces or salsas can make authentic-tasting accompaniments for main courses. They can also be served with any of the light meals, so making them more substantial. Vegetables served in sauces made from nuts, seeds or avocados are very popular and they can be turned into light supper dishes themselves if the ingredients are doubled. As well as vegetable or salad dishes, cooked beans are always served with the Mexican main course.

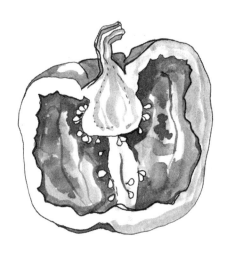

Roasted vegetables *(serves 4)*

8oz/225g courgette, halved lengthwise and sliced

4oz/100g red pepper, chopped

4oz/100g orange pepper, chopped

4oz/100g button mushrooms, wiped

4oz/100g tomato, cut into wedges

1 red onion, peeled and sliced

2 garlic cloves, finely sliced

1 green chilli, finely sliced

1 tablespoon olive oil

1 bay leaf

1 sprig of fresh thyme, chopped

black pepper

toasted pine kernels

Heat the oil and fry the onion, garlic and chilli until softened. Remove from the heat and add the remaining ingredients apart from the pine kernels. Mix together well, then transfer to a shallow baking dish. Bake in a preheated oven at 180°C/350°F/Gas mark 4 for about 35 minutes until the vegetables are just tender. Garnish with toasted pine kernels.

Chilli potatoes *(serves 4)*

1lb12oz/800g potatoes, peeled and diced

8oz/225g tomato, skinned and chopped

1 medium red onion, peeled and finely chopped

1 garlic clove, crushed

1 dessertspoon corn oil

1 dessertspoon tomato purée

1 tablespoon finely chopped fresh coriander

1 teaspoon chilli powder

black pepper

1oz/25g vegan 'cheese', grated

1 small green chilli, finely chopped

fresh coriander leaves

Soften the onion and garlic in the oil. Add the tomato, tomato purée, tablespoonful of chopped coriander and chilli powder, season with black pepper and stir well. Bring to the boil and simmer gently, while stirring occasionally, for 10 minutes. Meanwhile put the potatoes in a large pan of water, bring to the boil, cover and simmer until cooked. Mash the tomato in the sauce with the back of a spoon, then drain the cooked potatoes and add them to the hot sauce. Mix well and spoon into a warmed serving dish. Sprinkle the grated 'cheese' and chopped chilli on the top and garnish with coriander leaves.

Fried potatoes with mushrooms (serves 4)

1½lb/675g potatoes, peeled

4oz/100g mushrooms, wiped and finely chopped

1 small onion, peeled and finely chopped

½ green chilli, finely chopped

1 garlic clove, crushed

1 tablespoon corn oil

black pepper

1oz/25g vegan 'cheese', grated

chopped fresh parsley

Cut the potatoes into even-sized chunks and boil until almost done. Drain and chop finely. Heat the oil and gently fry the onion, chilli and garlic until soft. Add the mushrooms and fry until the juices begin to run, then add the potatoes and season with black pepper. Mix well and continue cooking for 5 minutes whilst stirring. Transfer to a warmed ovenproof dish and sprinkle the 'cheese' on top. Place briefly under a hot grill until the 'cheese' starts to melt. Serve garnished with chopped parsley.

Potato with leek and avocado   *(serves 4)*

> 1½lb/675g potatoes, scraped
>
> 8oz/225g leek, trimmed and finely sliced
>
> 1 small avocado, peeled and mashed
>
> 4 fl.oz/125ml soya milk
>
> 1 dessertspoon corn oil
>
> ½ green chilli, finely chopped
>
> black pepper
>
> chopped fresh coriander leaves

Cook the potatoes, drain and dice. Heat the oil and soften the leek and chilli. Remove from the heat and add the avocado and soya milk, season with black pepper and stir well. Add the potatoes and mix thoroughly. Transfer to a baking dish, cover and bake in a preheated oven at 180°C/350°F/Gas mark 4 for 25 minutes. Garnish with chopped coriander when serving.

Creamed potato with avocado   *(serves 4)*

> 2lb/900g potatoes, peeled
>
> 1 medium avocado, peeled and mashed
>
> 1 tablespoon vegan margarine
>
> 2 tablespoons soya milk
>
> 1 teaspoon parsley
>
> black pepper
>
> finely chopped green chilli

Cut the potatoes into even-sized chunks and boil until cooked, then drain and dry off over a low heat. Mash the potatoes with the margarine. Stir in the avocado, soya milk and parsley, season with black pepper and mix thoroughly. Spoon the mixture into an ovenproof dish and fork the top over. Cover and place in a preheated oven at 180°C/350°F/Gas mark 4 for 10 minutes until heated through. Garnish with chopped green chilli.

Sweet potato and chickpea mole *(serves 4/6)*

2lb/900g sweet potatoes, peeled and diced

8oz/225g cooked chickpeas

½ quantity mole sauce (see page 42)

toasted sesame seeds

Cook the potatoes until just done. Heat the chickpeas in boiling water until hot. Meanwhile, heat the mole sauce, whilst stirring, until hot. Drain the potatoes and chickpeas and add to the sauce, mixing together. Transfer to a warmed serving dish and garnish with toasted sesame seeds.

Courgettes with mushrooms *(serves 4)*

12oz/350g courgettes, halved lengthwise and sliced

12oz/350g tomato, skinned and chopped

8oz/225g button mushrooms, wiped and halved

1 red onion, peeled and sliced

2 garlic cloves, crushed

1 red chilli, finely chopped

1 tablespoon olive oil

1 teaspoon dried oregano

few drops tabasco sauce

black pepper

chopped fresh parsley

Heat the oil and gently fry the onion, garlic and chilli until softened. Add the tomato and fry until pulpy. Stir in the courgettes, oregano and tabasco sauce and season with black pepper. Simmer gently until the courgettes are nearly tender, then add the mushrooms and continue cooking for another minute or two. Transfer to a warmed dish and serve garnished with fresh parsley.

Sweetcorn and pepper medley *(serves 4)*

8oz/225g sweetcorn kernels

4oz/100g green pepper, finely chopped

4oz/100g red pepper, finely chopped

2oz/50g mushrooms, wiped and finely chopped

2oz/50g tomato, skinned and chopped

1 small red onion, peeled and finely chopped

1 garlic clove, crushed

½ small red chilli, finely chopped

1 tablespoon olive oil

1 rounded tablespoon finely chopped fresh herbs

black pepper

1 tomato, cut into wedges

Fry the green and red peppers, onion, garlic and chilli in the oil until soft. Add the remaining ingredients and stir well. Continue cooking for a few minutes more until the vegetables are done. Spoon into a serving dish and garnish with the tomato wedges.

Cauliflower with chickpeas in avocado sauce

(serves 4)

1lb/450g cauliflower, cut into florets

4oz/100g cooked chickpeas

1 medium avocado, peeled and mashed

1 onion, peeled and finely chopped

1 garlic clove, crushed

½ green chilli, finely chopped

1 dessertspoon corn oil

1 rounded tablespoon finely chopped fresh parsley

8 fl.oz/225ml vegetable stock

6 fl.oz/175ml soya milk

1 rounded dessertspoon cornflour

black pepper

chopped fresh coriander leaves

Heat the oil in a large pan and gently fry the onion, garlic and chilli until softened. Add the cauliflower, stock and parsley and season with black pepper. Mix well and bring to the boil, then cover and simmer gently until the liquid is reduced and the cauliflower is just tender. Mix the cornflour with the soya milk until smooth and add to the pan together with the chickpeas and mashed avocado. Stir well and bring to the boil while stirring. Simmer for a couple of minutes until the sauce thickens. Transfer to a warmed serving dish and garnish with chopped coriander.

Broccoli with mushrooms in walnut sauce

(serves 4)

8oz/225g broccoli, chopped

8oz/225g mushrooms, wiped and finely chopped

1oz/25g walnuts, ground

1 onion, peeled and finely chopped

1 garlic clove, crushed

1 green chilli, finely chopped

1 tablespoon corn oil

2 tablespoons finely chopped fresh coriander leaves

5 fl.oz/150ml vegetable stock

4 fl.oz/125ml soya milk

1 rounded dessertspoon cornflour

black pepper

chopped walnuts

Fry the onion, garlic and chilli in the oil until softened. Add the mushrooms and fry until the juices begin to run. Now add the broccoli, coriander and stock and season with black pepper. Bring to the boil and simmer gently until the broccoli is just cooked. Mix the cornflour with the soya milk until smooth and add to the pan together with the ground walnuts. Bring to the boil while stirring and continue stirring for a minute or two until the sauce thickens. Serve in a warmed dish garnished with chopped walnuts.

Chayote and cauliflower with green pepper and pumpkin seed sauce *(serves 4)*

2 chayotes, peeled and chopped

6oz/175g cauliflower, cut into small florets

pumpkin seeds

sauce

4oz/100g green pepper, chopped

1oz/25g pumpkin seeds

1 small onion, peeled and chopped

1 garlic clove, chopped

1 green chilli, finely chopped

1 slice of French bread, broken into small pieces

1 tablespoon corn oil

1 tablespoon chopped fresh parsley

black pepper

6 fl.oz/175ml vegetable stock

Heat the oil and gently fry the green pepper, onion, garlic and chilli for 5 minutes. Add the 1oz/25g pumpkin seeds and the French bread and fry for a further 2 minutes while stirring. Stir in the stock and parsley and season with black pepper. Bring to the boil, cover and simmer for 5 minutes, then remove from the heat and allow to cool slightly before blending smooth in a blender. Pour the sauce back into the cleaned pan. Steam the chayote and cauliflower separately until tender. Meanwhile reheat the sauce while stirring, then add the cooked vegetables. Spoon into a warmed serving dish and garnish with pumpkin seeds.

SALADS

Mexicans are very fond of salads and they are often served as accompaniments for more fiery main courses. A wide variety of ingredients is used to make up colourful and nutritious bowls and platters and those containing beans are especially popular. Salads of red, white and green ingredients (the colours of the Mexican flag) are traditionally served on Mexican Independence Day. Light meals are also served with a salad garnish, and the salad becomes a meal in itself when piled high on a tortilla and garnished with salsa.

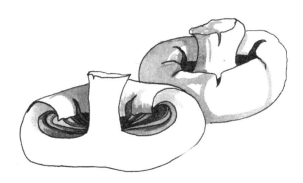

Celebration salad platter

Variations of this colourful and appetising salad are traditionally served on Christmas Eve. It can be made as big or as small as you wish and served as an accompaniment or as a buffet platter. The ingredients can be varied according to what's in season.

selection of red and green lettuce leaves, shredded

beetroot slices

avocado slices

pinceapple cubes

green-skinned apple slices

banana slices

papaya slices

radish halves

red onion rings

cucumber slices

cherry tomato halves

lemon juice

pine kernels

pomegranate seeds

dressing

5 tablespoons olive oil

2 tablespoons white wine vinegar

1 tablespoon lime juice

black pepper

Sprinkle the avocado, apple and banana slices with lemon juice. Spread the shredded lettuce on a serving platter. Whisk the dressing ingredients together until well combined. Arrange the salad ingredients in rows on the lettuce and drizzle the dressing over the top. Garnish with pine kernels and pomegranate seeds.

Avocado and sweetcorn salad   *(serves 6)*

2 small or 1 large avocado, peeled and diced

8oz/225g sweetcorn kernels

4oz/100g cooked red kidney beans

4oz/100g red pepper, chopped

2oz/50g mushrooms, wiped and chopped

2oz/50g red onion, peeled and finely chopped

1 garlic clove, crushed

1 tablespoon chopped capers

1 tablespoon white wine vinegar

1 dessertspoon lemon juice

1 dessertspoon olive oil

dash of tabasco sauce

black pepper

shredded lettuce leaves

pumpkin seeds

finely chopped fresh parsley

Blanch the sweetcorn kernels, drain and rinse under cold running water. Put them in a mixing bowl and add the kidney beans, red pepper, mushrooms, onion, garlic, capers and avocado. Mix the vinegar with the lemon juice, olive oil and tabasco and spoon over the salad. Season with black pepper and toss well. Arrange some shredded lettuce on a serving plate and pile the salad on top. Serve garnished with pumpkin seeds and chopped parsley.

Mixed bean salad   *(serves 4/6)*

12oz/350g cooked mixed beans (e.g. red kidney, borlotti, pinto, black)

4oz/100g shelled broad beans

4oz/100g green beans, topped, tailed and cut into 1/2 inch/1cm
lengths

½ quantity tomato sauce (see page 41)

4 spring onions, trimmed and finely chopped

4 green olives, chopped

1 tablespoon finely chopped red chilli

chopped fresh coriander leaves

Steam the broad and green beans until just tender. Rinse in cold water, then slip the skins from the broad beans and discard. Put all ingredients apart from the coriander in a bowl and mix thoroughly. Transfer to a serving bowl, cover and chill. Garnish with chopped coriander when serving.

Mushroom salad   *(serves 4)*

1lb/450g mushrooms, wiped and sliced

1 small onion, peeled and finely chopped

1 red chilli, finely chopped

2 garlic cloves, crushed

2 tablespoons olive oil

2 tablespoons finely chopped fresh coriander

1 dessertspoon lemon juice

black pepper

shredded lettuce leaves

6 green olives, chopped

Heat the oil and gently fry the onion, chilli and garlic until soft. Add the mushrooms, coriander and lemon juice and season with black pepper. Stir well and fry for a few minutes more until the juices begin to run. Refrigerate until cold, then pile the mushrooms on a bed of shredded lettuce. Garnish with chopped olives.

Green and orange salad *(serves 4)*

    1 large bowl of prepared mixed green salad ingredients (e.g.
        shredded crisp lettuce, tender spinach leaves, watercress,
        cucumber)
    1 large avocado, peeled and chopped
    1 orange
    1 dessertspoon olive oil
    1 dessertspoon white wine vinegar
    1 tablespoon fresh orange juice
    1 tablespoon finely chopped fresh coriander leaves
    black pepper
    1 tablespoon chopped pecans

Peel the orange and keep a piece of peel. Chop the orange segments after removing the membranes, pith and seeds. Drain and add the orange to the green salad, together with the avocado and fresh coriander. Mix the olive oil with the vinegar and orange juice and pour over the salad, then season with black pepper and toss very well. Transfer to a serving bowl and sprinkle the chopped pecans on top. Finely grate the piece of orange peel and use this as garnish.

Chickpea and pepper salad *(serves 4)*

    8oz/225g cooked chickpeas
    8oz/225g mixed peppers, finely chopped
    4oz/100g ripe tomato, skinned and finely chopped
    1 small red onion, skinned and finely chopped
    1 garlic clove, crushed
    6 green olives, chopped
    1 tablespoon finely chopped fresh coriander leaves

1 dessertspoon olive oil

1 tablespoon white wine vinegar

1 teaspoon lemon juice

few drops tabasco sauce

black pepper

Put the chickpeas, peppers, tomato, onion, garlic, olives and coriander in a bowl, season with black pepper and mix. Combine the olive oil with the vinegar, lemon juice and tabasco sauce. Spoon this dressing over the salad and toss thoroughly. Transfer to a serving bowl and chill before serving.

Potato and broad bean salad   *(serves 4)*

1lb/450g potatoes, scraped

8oz/225g shelled broad beans

shredded crisp lettuce leaves

finely sliced spring onions

1 garlic clove, crushed

1 dessertspoon olive oil

1 dessertspoon lemon juice

1 dessertspoon white wine vinegar

½ teaspoon dried parsley

black pepper

Boil the potatoes until just done, drain and allow to cool, then dice them and put them in a mixing bowl. Cook the broad beans until tender, drain and rinse under cold running water. Slip the skins from the beans and add the beans to the potato. Mix the olive oil with the garlic, lemon juice, vinegar and parsley, season with black pepper and spoon over the salad. Toss carefully, then cover and chill. Arrange some shredded lettuce on a serving plate and pile the salad on top. Garnish with finely sliced spring onions.

Vegetable and pinto bean salad   *(serves 4)*

> 6oz/175g cooked pinto beans
>
> 4oz/100g courgette, sliced
>
> 4oz/100g green pepper, chopped
>
> 4oz/100g red pepper, chopped
>
> 4oz/100g green beans, topped, tailed and cut into 1 inch/2.5cm lengths
>
> 4oz/100g mushrooms, wiped and chopped
>
> 1 red onion, peeled and sliced
>
> 1 green chilli, chopped
>
> 1 garlic clove, crushed
>
> 1 tablespoon olive oil
>
> ½ quantity tomato sauce (see page 41)
>
> chopped fresh coriander leaves
>
> toasted pine kernels

Blanch the green beans briefly, just to soften them slightly, then refresh under cold running water. Drain well and put in a bowl with the pinto beans. Heat the oil and gently fry the courgette, green and red peppers and onion until softened but not cooked. Remove from the heat and stir in the chilli, garlic and mushrooms, then add to the beans and mix. Pour the tomato sauce over the salad and combine well. Transfer to a serving dish, cover and chill. Serve garnished with chopped coriander and pine kernels.

Chayote and green bean salad   *(serves 4)*

> 2 chayotes, peeled and chopped
>
> 8oz/225g green beans, topped, tailed and cut into ½ inch/1cm lengths
>
> 2oz/50g cucumber, chopped

1 green chilli, finely chopped

8 spring onions, trimmed and finely sliced

2 garlic cloves, crushed

1 dessertspoon lime juice

1 dessertspoon olive oil

1 dessertspoon white wine vinegar

pinch of ground bay leaves

black pepper

mixed salad leaves

1 rounded tablespoon finely chopped fresh coriander leaves

pomegranate seeds

Blanch the chayote and green beans for 2 minutes, then rinse in cold water. Drain and put in a large bowl with the chilli, cucumber, spring onions and coriander. Mix the lime juice with the olive oil, vinegar, ground bay leaves and garlic and season with black pepper. Add to the salad and mix thoroughly. Arrange some salad leaves on a serving plate and pile the salad on top. Garnish with pomegranate seeds, cover and chill before serving.

DESSERTS

A cool, refreshing fruit salad made from the wide range of tropical fruits that are grown in or around the region is sometimes all that is required after a fiery and filling Mexican meal. Tropical fruits are also used as the basis for a multitude of sorbets, ice creams, jellies and custards. Tortillas inevitably find their way into dessert recipes as well, with wheat tortillas being used in a variety of ways to enclose fruit fillings, while sweetened corn tortilla chips are often served with fruit salads. These are easily made by frying the 'chips' in the usual way and then shaking them in a mixture of demerara sugar and ground cinnamon. Tamales and empanadas can also be made into desserts by using fruit mixtures instead of savoury fillings. Pumpkin may seem an unusual choice for dessert, but many Mexicans are very fond of this vegetable, especially when it is cooked in a syrup made from sugar, fruit juice and cinnamon.

Tropical fruit salad   *(serves 4)*

14oz/400g tin guavas in syrup

1 mango, peeled and diced

1 papaya, peeled and diced

¼ small melon, peeled and diced

1 passion fruit

1 dessertspoon lime juice

1 tablespoon tequila (optional)

pomegranate seeds

Chop the guavas and put them in a mixing bowl with the mango, papaya and melon. Scoop the seeds and flesh from the passion fruit and add together with the lime juice and tequila. Combine everything well, then cover and chill for a couple of hours. Transfer to a serving bowl and garnish with pomegranate seeds.

Citrus jelly bowls   *(serves 4)*

1 grapefruit

1 large orange

demerara sugar

15 fl.oz/450ml fresh orange juice

1 rounded teaspoon agar agar

Peel the grapefruit and orange and remove the pith, membranes and pips. Chop the segments and put them in a bowl. Add a little demerara sugar to sweeten and mix well. Keep some of the fruit for garnish and divide the rest between 4 serving bowls. Dissolve the agar agar in the orange juice and heat gently, whilst stirring, to just below boiling point. Pour over the fruit in the bowls, then cover and refrigerate for a few hours until set. Garnish with the remaining fruit when serving.

Pineapple and rum sorbet   *(serves 4)*

    12oz/350g fresh pineapple flesh, chopped

    10 fl.oz/300ml water

    1oz/25g demerara sugar

    2 tablespoons dark rum

Put the pineapple, water and sugar in a saucepan and bring to the boil. Simmer for 2 minutes, then allow to cool slightly. Add the rum and blend until smooth. Pour the mixture into a shallow freezerproof container, cover and freeze for 1 hour. Whisk and return to the freezer for a few hours until just frozen. Keep at room temperature for 45 minutes before serving if the sorbet has become too solid.

Lemon and lime sorbet   *(serves 4)*

    2 lemons

    1 lime

    2oz/50g caster sugar

    water

    1 rounded teaspoon agar agar

Squeeze the juice from the lemons and lime and pour it, together with any bits of flesh, into a measuring jug. Make up to 12 fl.oz/350ml with water. Pour into a small saucepan and add the agar agar. Stir well until dissolved, then add the sugar. Heat gently while stirring to just below boiling point. Pour into a freezerproof container, cover and freeze for 1 hour. Whisk thoroughly, then return to the freezer for another hour and whisk again. Put back in the freezer for a few hours until just frozen. If the sorbet has become too hard keep it at room temperature for 45 minutes, before serving with fresh fruit.

Banana and chocolate ice   *(serves 4)*

1 large ripe banana (approx. 8oz./225g), peeled and mashed

1oz/25g vegan chocolate, grated

9 fl.oz/250ml soya 'cream'

Whisk all the ingredients together and pour them into a freezerproof container. Cover and freeze for 1 hour, then whisk thoroughly. Return to the freezer until just frozen and serve with fresh fruit. Keep at room temperature for 45 minutes before serving if it is too hard.

Pineapple custard   *(serves 4)*

1lb/450g fresh pineapple flesh, chopped

10 fl.oz/300ml soya milk

1oz/25g cornflour

1oz/25g demerara sugar

grated vegan chocolate

Strain any juice from the pineapple and keep 2 fl.oz/50ml of this. Divide half of the pineapple between 4 serving glasses. Put the rest in a saucepan with the juice and the sugar. Bring to the boil and simmer for 5 minutes. Dissolve the cornflour in the soya milk and pour into a blender. Add the cooked pineapple and remaining juice and blend until smooth. Transfer to a double boiler and bring to the boil while stirring. Continue stirring for a minute or two until the custard thickens, then pour it over the pineapple in the glasses. Cover and refrigerate for a few hours until set. Sprinkle grated chocolate on top when serving.

Mango ice cream   *(serves 6/8)*

    1 large firm mango, peeled and chopped
    2oz/50g demerara sugar
    2 fl.oz/50ml water
    1 tablespoon lemon juice
    9 fl.oz/250ml soya 'cream'

Put the mango, sugar, water and lemon juice in a saucepan and cook gently until soft. Allow to cool, then transfer to a blender. Add the 'cream' and blend until smooth. Pour into a shallow freezerproof container, cover and freeze for 2 hours. Whisk the mixture and return it to the freezer for a few hours more until just frozen. Keep at room temperature for 45 minutes before serving if the ice cream becomes too hard.

Crème caramel   *(serves 4)*

    2oz/50g demerara sugar
    16 fl.oz/475ml soya milk
    1 teaspoon vanilla essence
    3 tablespoons water
    2 rounded tablespoons cornflour
    extra demerara sugar

Mix the cornflour and vanilla essence with the soya milk until smooth, then pour into a saucepan and heat gently, but do not allow it to boil. Put the 2oz/50g sugar into another saucepan and heat gently until the sugar caramelises, stirring frequently to prevent sticking. Remove from the heat and add the warmed milk mixture. Whisk thoroughly until well combined, pour into a double boiler and bring to the boil while stirring. Continue stirring for a minute or two until the sauce thickens. Pass the sauce through a sieve into a jug, then pour it into 4 3 inch/8cm ramekin dishes. Cover and chill for a few hours until set. Sprinkle the crème with demerara sugar and place the dishes under a hot grill until the sugar caramelises. Put back in the fridge until cold before serving.

Banana and date chimichangas   *(serves 4)*

 4 wheat tortillas (see page 21)
 2 bananas, peeled and chopped
 4oz/100g dried dates, finely chopped
 4 fl.oz/125ml fresh orange juice
 ¼ teaspoon ground cinnamon
 1 rounded tablespoon vegan margarine

Put the dates, orange juice and cinnamon in a small pan and simmer gently until the juice has been absorbed and the dates are soft. Remove from the heat and mash the dates with the back of a spoon, then stir in the chopped bananas.

Wrap the tortillas in foil and place them in a warm oven for a few minutes to soften. Divide the filling between the warmed tortillas, putting it neatly in the centre. Fold the sides of the tortillas towards the centre to enclose the filling and make square parcels. Melt the margarine in a non-stick frying pan. Carefully transfer the chimichangas to the pan and fry for a few minutes on each side until golden brown. Serve hot with vegan ice cream.

Sopapillas   *(serves 4)*

<u>pastry</u>
8oz/225g plain flour
1oz/25g vegan margarine
1 rounded teaspoon baking powder

½ teaspoon salt

approx. 4 fl.oz/125ml warm water

corn oil

syrup

1oz/25g vegan margarine

½oz/15g demerara sugar

2 tablespoons dark rum or fruit juice

½ teaspoon ground cinnamon

Sift the flour with the salt and baking powder. Rub in the margarine and gradually add enough water to form a soft dough. Turn out onto a floured board and knead well. Roll out to a 9 inch/23cm square and cut this into 9 3 inch/8cm squares. Shallow fry the squares in hot oil for a few minutes on each side until golden. Drain on kitchen paper.

Put the ingredients for the syrup in a non-stick frying pan and heat gently until well combined. Cut each of the pastry squares into 4 triangles and add them to the syrup. Cook for a few minutes, turning the triangles over, until they are all coated in syrup. Serve hot with fresh fruit.

Coconut rice pudding   (serves 4)

4oz/100g long grain rice

1oz/25g desiccated coconut

1oz/25g demerara sugar

1oz/25g sultanas, chopped

¼ teaspoon ground cinnamon

8 fl.oz/225ml water

10 fl.oz/300ml soya milk

toasted flaked coconut

Bring the rice and water to the boil, cover and simmer gently until the water has been absorbed. Remove from the heat and stir in the remaining ingredients apart from the flaked coconut. Stir until well combined, then return to the heat and bring back to the boil. Lower the heat and cook very gently, stirring occasionally, until the milk has been absorbed and the mixture is thick. Spoon into bowls and serve warm, garnished with toasted flaked coconut.

Chocolate and pecan pots *(serves 4)*

20 fl.oz/600ml soya milk

2oz/50g demerara sugar

1oz/25g cocoa powder

1oz/25g cornflour

1 teaspoon vanilla essence

chopped pecans

grated vegan chocolate

Whisk the cocoa powder, cornflour, sugar and vanilla with the soya milk until smooth. Transfer to a double boiler and bring to the boil while stirring. Continue stirring for a minute or two until the mixture thickens. Pour into 4 serving glasses, cover and chill for a few hours until set. Top each dessert with chopped pecans and grated chocolate.

Banana mocha pots *(serves 4)*

2 bananas

lemon juice

16 fl.oz/475ml soya milk

1oz/25g cornflour

1 dessertspoon coffee powder or granules

1 dessertspoon cocoa powder

1 rounded tablespoon demerara sugar

½ teaspoon vanilla essence

chopped walnuts

grated vegan chocolate

Peel and chop the bananas and sprinkle with a little lemon juice. Divide between 4 serving glasses. Dissolve the cornflour, coffee, cocoa, sugar and vanilla in the soya milk and pour into a double boiler. Bring to the boil while stirring, then continue stirring for a minute or two until the sauce thickens. Pour the sauce over the bananas, cover and refrigerate for a few hours until set. Garnish with chopped walnuts and grated chocolate.

Mexican bread pudding   *(serves 4)*

8oz/225g tin chopped pineapple in natural juice

4oz/100g French bread, cut into thin slices

2oz/50g vegan 'cream cheese'

1oz/25g desiccated coconut

1oz/25g raisins, chopped

½oz/15g demerara sugar

5 tablespoons soya milk

½ teaspoon ground cinnamon

vegan margarine

finely chopped pecans

Spread the slices of bread with margarine and cut them into cubes. Mix the 'cream cheese' with the coconut, raisins, sugar, cinnamon, pineapple and juice from the tin. Add the bread cubes and combine until well coated. Transfer to a greased baking dish and spoon the soya milk evenly over the top. Sprinkle with chopped pecans and bake in a preheated oven at 180°C/350°F/Gas mark 4 for about 25 minutes until golden brown. Serve hot.

BAKING

*It may come as a surprise to find sweetcorn cropping up as an
ingredient in a cake recipe, but it is such a staple that Mexicans use it
at every opportunity in both savoury and sweet dishes. Other
ingredients will be more familiar from baking recipes from other
cuisines. Nuts feature regularly and cinnamon is a very popular spice,
used extensively to flavour biscuits and cakes. Pan dulce, a chocolate-
flavoured bread, is a favourite which is served with coffee throughout
the day, both in cafés and at home. Although tortillas are the main
'bread' of Mexico, cornbread and little white rolls called bolillos are
equally popular in many households. When served warm both of these
make excellent accompaniments for soups and main courses.*

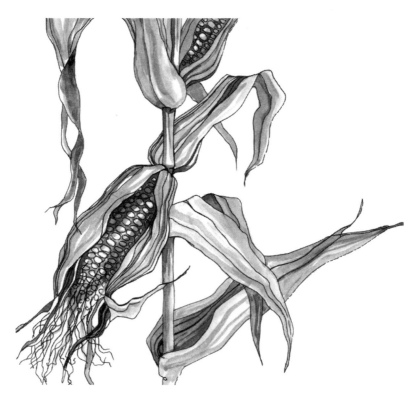

Cornbread $(serves\ 9)$

8oz/225g self-raising flour

4oz/100g cornmeal

3oz/75g vegan margarine, melted

1 small onion, peeled and grated

1 small red chilli, finely chopped

¼ teaspoon salt

10 fl.oz/300ml soya milk

Mix the flour with the cornmeal, onion, chilli and salt, add the melted margarine and combine well. Gradually add the soya milk and stir thoroughly. Spoon the mixture into a lined and greased 7 inch/18cm square baking tin. Level the top and bake in a preheated oven at 190°C/375°F/Gas mark 5 for about 25 minutes until golden. Carefully turn out of the tin, cut into squares and serve warm.

Bolillos $(makes\ 12)$

1lb/450g plain flour

1 sachet easy-blend yeast

1 teaspoon salt

approx. 10 fl.oz/300ml soya milk, warmed

extra soya milk

sesame seeds

Sift the flour with the yeast and salt into a mixing bowl and gradually add the warmed soya milk until a soft dough forms. Turn out onto a floured board and knead for 5 minutes. Return the dough to the bowl, cover and leave in a warm place for an hour until risen. Knead the dough again for 5 minutes, then divide it into 12 equal portions. Roll each portion into a fat 'sausage' shape and put them on a greased baking sheet. Make a couple of slits in the top of each roll and leave them in a warm place for 45 minutes to rise. Brush the tops with soya milk and sprinkle with sesame seeds. Bake in a preheated oven at 180°C/350°F/Gas mark 4 for about 15 minutes until golden brown. Serve warm or cold.

Pan dulce

1lb/450g plain flour

2oz/50g sultanas, chopped

2oz/50g raisins, chopped

2oz/50g vegan margarine, melted

2oz/50g demerara sugar

1oz/25g walnuts, finely chopped

1oz/25g cocoa powder

1 sachet easy-blend yeast

approx. 8 fl.oz/225ml soya milk, warmed

2 tablespoons dark rum or fruit juice

½ teaspoon ground cinnamon

Put the sultanas, raisins, cinnamon and rum or fruit juice in a bowl and stir well. Cover and leave to soak for 2 hours. Sift the flour with the cocoa and yeast, stir in the sugar and walnuts, then add the soaked fruit and melted margarine. Mix together well and gradually add the soya milk until a soft dough forms. Turn out onto a floured board and knead well. Return to the bowl, cover and leave to rise in a warm place for 1 hour. Knead the dough again, then shape it into a ball. Flatten this slightly and place it on a greased baking sheet. Cut a cross shape on the top with a sharp knife. Leave in a warm place to rise again for 45 minutes. Bake in a preheated oven at 190°C/375°F/Gas mark 5 for 20-25 minutes, until the bread sounds hollow when tapped underneath. Transfer to a wire rack and allow to cool. Cut into slices to serve.

Sultana and cinnamon bread ring

8oz/225g plain flour

1oz/25g demerara sugar

1oz/25g vegan margarine, melted

1 dessertspoon easy-blend yeast

½ teaspoon salt

approx. 3 fl.oz/75ml warm water

4oz/100g sultanas

2 tablespoons fruit juice

1 teaspoon ground cinnamon

soya milk

sesame seeds

Mix the flour, sugar, yeast and salt in a large bowl, add the melted margarine and combine well. Gradually add the warm water until a soft dough forms. Turn out onto a floured board and knead thoroughly. Return to the bowl, cover and leave in a warm place for 1 hour to rise.

Put the sultanas, fruit juice and cinnamon in a small saucepan and simmer gently until the juice has been absorbed. Allow to cool.

Turn the dough out onto a floured board and knead again. Shape or roll into an oblong of 11 x 7 inches/28 x 18cm. Spread the fruit lengthwise along the centre of the dough, then fold the two long edges over to enclose it. Gently press on the top of the dough to force out any air. Form the dough into a ring and place it on a greased baking tray. Leave for 45 minutes in a warm place to rise, then brush the top with soya milk and sprinkle with sesame seeds. Bake in a preheated oven at 200°C/400°F/Gas mark 6 for 15-20 minutes until browned. Slide onto a wire rack and allow to cool before cutting into wedges.

Wedding cakes *(makes 20)*

4oz/100g plain flour

4oz/100g vegan margarine

2oz/50g caster sugar

2oz/50g walnuts, grated

1oz/25g cornflour

¼ teaspoon ground cinnamon

Cream the margarine with the sugar, then work in the sifted flour, cornflour and cinnamon and the walnuts. Take heaped teaspoonfuls of the mixture and roll into balls with dampened hands. Put them on a greased baking sheet and flatten each ball slightly, allowing space between them for spreading. Bake in a preheated oven at 180°C/350°F/Gas mark 4 for 20-25 minutes until golden. Leave on the baking sheet for 10 minutes, then transfer to a wire rack to cool completely.

Cinnamon crunchies *(makes 18)*

8oz/225g plain flour

4oz/100g vegan margarine

2oz/50g demerara sugar

1 teaspoon ground cinnamon

1 teaspoon vanilla essence

2 tablespoons soya milk

to finish

1oz/25g demerara sugar

1 teaspoon ground cinnamon

Cream the margarine with the 2oz/50g sugar, the cinnamon and the vanilla. Work in the flour, then add the soya milk and combine until the mixture binds together. Mix the remaining sugar with the cinnamon in a little bowl. Take rounded dessertspoonfuls of the mixture and roll into balls in the palm of the hand. Roll each ball in the sugar and cinnamon mixture until coated all over, then flatten them and put them on a greased baking sheet, allowing room for spreading. Bake in a preheated oven at 180°C/350°F/Gas mark 4 for about 20 minutes until golden brown. Carefully transfer to a wire rack and allow to cool.

Coffee and pecan cookies *(makes approx. 18)*

3oz/75g plain flour

2oz/50g vegan margarine

1oz/25g demerara sugar

1oz/25g pecans, grated

1oz/25g cornflour

½ teaspoon vanilla essence

1 rounded dessertspoon coffee granules or powder

2 tablespoons soya milk

pecan pieces

Cream the margarine with the sugar, vanilla essence and coffee, work in the grated pecans and cornflour and add the flour and soya milk. Mix thoroughly until a soft dough forms. Turn out onto a floured board and roll out to approximately ¼ inch/5mm thick. Cut into 2¼inch/5.5cm circles with a biscuit cutter. Gather up the remaining dough and re-roll and cut until all used up. Put the circles on a greased baking sheet and press a pecan piece in the top of each one. Bake in a preheated oven at 180°C/350°F/Gas mark 4 for 10-12 minutes until browned. Leave the cookies on the baking sheet for 10 minutes before carefully transferring them to a wire rack.

Corn and sultana cake (serves 8)

4oz/100g sweetcorn kernels

5 fl.oz/150ml soya milk

2oz/50g vegan margarine

2oz/50g demerara sugar

2oz/50g sultanas, chopped

2oz/50g masa harina

4oz/100g plain flour

1 rounded teaspoon baking powder

Blanch and drain the sweetcorn, then put it in a blender with the soya milk and blend until smooth. Cream the margarine with the sugar, add the blended sweetcorn and the masa harina and mix well. Stir in the sultanas, then add the sifted flour and baking powder and combine thoroughly. Spoon the mixture into a lined and greased 7 inch/18cm round baking tin and level the top. Bake in a preheated oven at 180°C/350°F/Gas mark 4 for 35-40 minutes until golden. Carefully turn out onto a wire rack to cool. Cut into wedges to serve.

Chocolate and almond torta (serves 8)

3oz/75g plain flour

2oz/50g ground almonds

2oz/50g vegan margarine

2oz/50g demerara sugar

½oz/15g cocoa powder

1 banana (about 6oz/175g) peeled and mashed

1 tablespoon dark rum

1 teaspoon almond essence

1 teaspoon baking powder

3 fl.oz/75ml soya milk

to finish

2oz/50g vegan chocolate bar, broken

toasted chopped flaked almonds

Cream the margarine with the sugar and almond essence in a mixing bowl. Stir in the banana and ground almonds. Add the sifted flour, cocoa powder and baking powder, then add the soya milk and rum and mix thoroughly. Spoon the mixture into a lined and greased 7 inch/18cm diameter baking tin. Level the top and bake in a preheated oven at 180°C/350°F/Gas mark 4 for 30 minutes. Carefully transfer to a wire rack and allow to cool.

Melt the chocolate in a bowl over a pan of boiling water. Spread the chocolate evenly over the torta and sprinkle the flaked almonds on top. Refrigerate for a couple of hours until the chocolate has set. Serve cut into wedges.

DRINKS

Stalls selling cold drinks made from blended fresh fruits are a familiar sight in many Mexican towns and villages. These healthy and delicious drinks are also made at home from virtually any soft fruit and they are always served at mealtimes. Both hot chocolate and coffee-based drinks are very popular and are drunk after meals and throughout the day. Coffee is always served black and a dash of coffee-flavoured liqueur is often added when it is served at the end of a meal. The national drink of Mexico is tequila, a potent spirit which is distilled from the juice of the agave tequilana, a fleshy-leaved plant which is native to the region.

Mango smoothie *(serves 4)*

    8oz/225g ripe mango flesh, diced

    20 fl.oz/600ml soya milk

    8 fl.oz/225ml water

    sugar (optional)

    crushed ice

Blend the mango with the soya milk and water, adding sugar if desired, until smooth. Pour into tumblers and add crushed ice.

Melon and lime crush *(serves 6)*

    8oz/225g ripe melon flesh, chopped

    2 tablespoons lime juice

    1 rounded tablespoon demerara sugar

    24 fl.oz/725ml water

    8 fl.oz/225ml soya milk

    crushed ice

    6 lime slices

Put the melon, lime juice, sugar, water and soya milk in a blender and blend until smooth. Pour into glasses and add crushed ice. Garnish each glass with a slice of lime.

Pineapple lemonade *(serves 4)*

    8oz/225g fresh pineapple flesh, chopped

    2 tablespoons lemon juice

    28 fl.oz/825ml water

2 rounded tablespoons granulated sugar

crushed ice

4 lemon slices

Bring the pineapple, lemon juice, water and sugar to the boil in a saucepan. Cover and simmer for 2 minutes. Allow to cool slightly, then blend smooth and pass through a strainer into a jug. Cover and refrigerate until cold. Remove any froth from the top and pour the lemonade into tumblers. Add crushed ice and garnish each glass with a slice of lemon.

Hot chocolate *(serves 4)*

3oz/75g vegan chocolate bar, broken

24 fl.oz/725ml soya milk

½ teaspoon vanilla essence

sugar (optional)

grated vegan chocolate

ground cinnamon

Put the broken chocolate, soya milk and vanilla essence in a saucepan, add a little sugar if desired and stir well. Slowly bring to the boil, whisking constantly until the chocolate has melted. Pour into mugs and sprinkle with grated chocolate and ground cinnamon.

Hot mocha *(serves 4)*

16 fl.oz/475ml soya milk

10 fl.oz/300ml water

1 rounded dessertspoon cocoa powder

1 rounded dessertspoon coffee granules

1 rounded dessertspoon demerara sugar

½ teaspoon vanilla essence

grated vegan chocolate

Mix all ingredients apart from the grated chocolate in a saucepan until smooth. Bring to the boil while whisking continuously, to create a frothy mixture. When the mixture has boiled pour into cups, spoon the froth on top and sprinkle with grated chocolate.

Mexican coffee   *(serves 4)*

2 dessertspoons coffee granules

2 dessertspoons cocoa powder

2 rounded dessertspoons demerara sugar

¼ teaspoon ground cinnamon

20 fl.oz/600ml water

Put the ingredients in a saucepan and stir until the coffee and cocoa dissolve. Bring to the boil and simmer for 30 seconds before serving.

Sangria   *(serves 6)*

1 bottle (25 fl.oz/750ml) red wine

10 fl.oz/300ml soda water

juice of 1 orange

ice cubes

chopped fresh strawberries

6 orange slices

Mix the wine with the soda water and orange juice. Pour into glasses and add ice cubes and chopped strawberries. Garnish each glass with a slice of orange.

Margarita *(serves 4)*

8 fl.oz/225ml tequila

2 fl.oz/50ml cointreau

1 lime

finely ground sea salt

crushed ice

Cut the lime in half and rub the flesh round the rims of the glasses. Put some salt on a plate and dip the glass rims in it until frosted. Squeeze the juice from the lime and blend with the tequila and cointreau and some crushed ice. Pour into the frosted glasses.

Strawberry sparkler *(serves 4)*

2oz/50g strawberries

10 fl.oz/300ml fresh orange juice

12 fl.oz/350ml sparkling white wine

extra strawberries, chopped

ice cubes

Blend the 2oz/50g strawberries with the orange juice until smooth. Pass through a sieve into a jug and add the sparkling wine. Mix well, then pour into glasses and add chopped strawberries and ice cubes.

More Vegan Cookbooks by Linda Majzlik

Vegan Dinner Parties

"If no one has yet told you that vegan food is varied, healthy and scrumptious, this is just the book for you. The author's choice of genuinely cruelty-free ingredients varies from the more exotic to the re-assuringly homely, but they all stimulate the taste buds and they're all available on the high street."

Vegan food is much in demand as more people are advised to avoid dairy products for health reasons. It is also a logical next choice after becoming a vegetarian, since meat is not the only animal product dependent on cruelty and abuse. So these recipes avoid the use of milk, butter, cream, honey and eggs, as well as meat and its by-products.

All the recipes are tried and tested. Although they are organised into monthly menus, you can of course pick and choose to make up menus and dishes for any occasion.

£5 paperback   96pp   1 897766 46 7

Illustrated with cartoons by Mark Blanford

"For the sake of the world, its people and its animals, it is important to reclaim our food from those who pretend that pain and suffering are an essential part of our diet. Enjoy these great recipes because they strike a blow for the oppressed of the world — humans and animals alike."

From the Foreword by Juliet Gellatley, founder and director of Viva!

Vegan Barbecues and Buffets

Having a barbecue on a hot summer's day? Laying on a buffet for a crowded event? The vegan choice is simply great!

From mushroom and pine kernel sausages and smoked tofu and mushroom medallions, a sunflower and soya loaf and aubergine and brazil nut paté to a tempting assortment of salads, spreads and dips, and an array of sumptuous desserts, Linda Majzlik takes you on a festive journey of vegan delights that will appeal to every palate, yet remains completely wholesome and cruelty-free from beginning to end.

A lot of the preparation can be done in advance: many of the recipes are suitable for freezing, while others can be kept in the fridge. So the cook can enjoy the day as much as the guests!

£5 paperback   96pp   1 897766 55 6

What they wrote about *Vegan Dinner Parties*:

'Imaginative... very good value' *The Vegan*

'Linda's tasty book runs through the twelve months of the year with a mouth-watering and well-balanced three-course meal for each one'
Wildlife Guardian

'This inspiring book proves just how sophisticated and tasty vegan food can be' *Agscene*

'Superb idea – a book long overdue' *Green World*

Vegan Baking

Includes over 100 recipes for cakes, loaves, biscuits, tray bakes, no-bake cakes and savoury baking – all free of animal products and all tried and tested.

£5 paperback   96pp   1 897766 63 7

'The book that every vegan has been waiting for …
the kind of cookery book that you wouildn't get bored with …
a very useful addition to any kitchen.' *The Vegan*

'Very good.' *The Vegetarian*

A Vegan Taste of the Caribbean

Appetisers, soups and stews, accompaniments for soups, stews and curries, main courses, rice, vegetables, salads, chutneys, salsas and sauces, desserts, baking, drinks. Over 100 recipes, plus what to keep in the Caribbean storecupboard.

'A taste of magic.' *The Vegetarian*

£5.99 paperback 112pp 1 897766 70 X

A Vegan Taste of Italy

Starters, soups, sauces, risottos, main courses (inlcuding stuffed vegetables, pizza, pasta, and vegeatbles), salads and desserts, and baking (Focaccia, breadsticks, panforte, macaroons, etc.). Over 120 recipes, all free of animal products.

'Over 120 recipes to delight and enthrall you.' *The Vegetarian*

£5.99 paperback 128pp 1 897766 65 3

A Vegan Taste of India

From snacks and starters, dhals and soups to breads and rice dishes, from salads and raitas to chutneys, desserts and drinks, the 120 recipes in this book remain true to the authentic flavours of India, but avoid animal ingredients.

£5.99 paperback 128pp 1 897766 75 0

Information on how to order can be found on the back of the
title page of this book.